# A MARRIAGE MADE IN HEAVEN

The Eternal Love of the Bride & Bridegroom

# A MARRIAGE MADE IN HEAVEN

## Glenn Greenwood
## Latayne C. Scott

WORD PUBLISHING
Dallas · London · Sydney · Singapore

A MARRIAGE MADE IN HEAVEN

Copyright © 1990 by Glenn Greenwood and Latayne C. Scott

**Library of Congress Cataloging in Publication Data**

Greenwood, Glenn, 1926–
    A marriage made in Heaven : the eternal love of the bride and bridegroom / by Glenn Greenwood and Latayne C. Scott.
      p.    cm.
    Includes bibliographical references.
    ISBN 0-8499-0782-9
    1. Church—Biblical teaching.  2. Jesus Christ—Person and offices.  3. Marriage—Biblical teaching.  I. Scott, Latayne Colvatt, 1952–   .  II. Title.
BS2417.C53G74   1990
262'.7—dc20                        90-36370
                                              CIP

*Printed in the United States of America*
0 1 2 3 4 9 BKC 9 8 7 6 5 4 3 2 1

Glenn dedicates this book
to his lovely wife

*Marge*

who has been a constant
source of encouragement
and inspiration in his ministry

Latayne dedicates this book
to her dear friend

*Melissa Harding*

# Contents

# *Preface*

Coauthoring a book is like a marriage. When you put two people of different backgrounds and abilities together, there is an inevitable amount of tension and excitement as well as the thrill of the unknown. But the "cause" is a worthwhile one, and we have given our best to make it succeed.

The "first person" of this book—the "I," if you will—is Glenn Greenwood, B.A., Th.B., M.Ed., D.D. His credentials, like his degrees, are impressive. He has spent thirty-four years of his life proclaiming God's Word, and twenty of those years have also been spent in public education as a teacher, administrator, and consultant.

His association with a Bible teacher who was well-versed in Bible customs sparked his interest in this same subject. Glenn's enthusiasm for this continued to grow and inevitably spilled over into his teachings. Soon he found himself to be a sought-after speaker on Bible customs, delivering messages on this theme all over the United States and in some twenty-five foreign countries.

His enthusiasm infected me, too! Our mutual prayer is that the readers of this book will fall in love, all over again, with our Spouse, the Lord Jesus Christ.

Latayne C. Scott

# Chapter 1

## *The Mystery of Marriage*

There was a festive atmosphere that night in Bangalore, India; and though I was tired from my schedule of speaking at four schools a day on this lecturing tour, I was nonetheless touched by the reception being held in my honor.

The president of the prestigious university hosting the reception was sitting at my right. Perhaps it was because I was leaning toward him, listening attentively, or maybe it was because of all the bustle and activity of the servants and waiters. At any rate, I did not pay much attention to the two women who were circling the dining room with basin and pitcher.

When they approached me, I looked up quickly. The person sitting to my left was wiping away the last drops of water from his hands. I plunged my hands into the basin of water and began to scrub them vigorously.

Conversation around me came to an awkward halt. The two servant women had horrified expressions on their faces. I immediately realized that I had done something very, very wrong. The president of the university motioned hurriedly to the two women, and I watched, embarrassed, as he held out his hands over the basin and allowed the woman with the pitcher to pour the cool, clean water over his hands.

I understood then that I had tried to wash my hands in the dirty water that had flowed off the hands of the other guests in the room: something akin to taking a busboy's table-cleaning rag and wiping one's mouth with it.

I was humbled as I allowed the woman to pour the water over

my hands, too. Two thoughts sprang into my mind. The first was the image of Elisha in 1 Kings 3:11, pouring a pitcher of water over the hands of Elijah, first to clean the prophet's hands, but also to show reverence to the great man. I knew then that what I had done was not only a hygienic faux pas. In a way, I had diminished the effect of what these Indian people were trying to show me. The ritual was carried out to show me I was welcome and honored in their presence and that they were servants ready to serve me.

The second thought was simply a realization of the obvious: I was not presently in America, and things were different here.

This situation is similar to the one in which any serious Bible student often finds himself. It is true that the Bible was written by men who were moved by the Holy Spirit—a Spirit who knows no cultural bounds. But the men through whom He worked were nonetheless citizens of the ancient Eastern world. As selective as these men were in the details they gave us, their individual person-alities, and their cultures, shine through their writings.

We are often confronted with the pitcher and basin of old customs described in the Bible. It is only by understanding these customs that we can fully appreciate the message of many of the most significant scriptures in the Bible.

This book is based on the premise that there is such a thing as absolute truth, and that it is revealed through God's Word. The messages and principles of the Bible are for all people, of all cultures and for all times. These truths are often couched in terms that tie them to customs and practices of long ago. Through these practices we can understand those principles. Many times Scripture is its own interpreter. That is, we know the meaning of such things as baptism and the Lord's Supper, because the Word explains them. Other times, though, the Bible student needs a little help in more fully understanding a custom. That's why writing this book has been such a joy for me. I want to share with you some of the exciting things I have learned about the marriage relationship.

I went through that phenomenon we call culture shock when I first took an around-the-world trip. But soon that disori-ented feeling gave way to one of fascination as I saw the many parallels to Bible customs being played out before my eyes in the homes and schools and marketplaces of the East. I began to realize that not only are the lives of Eastern people different, but also even their way of thinking is different. It is characteristic of the Oriental to brood long and deeply over a single concept, turning it over and over in his mind, exploring its possibilities and savoring its nuances. Then the truth is distilled and succinctly expressed in a few pungent, unforgettable words and images.

We can see this in the teachings of Jesus. Nowhere in any literature of the world are deeper concepts more indelibly expressed than in His seemingly simple parables. They have been repeatedly mined by generations and yield richer treasures with each new excavation.

Sometimes, though, we pass over the images of the Bible because we are confident that we understand all there is to know about them, and we are unwilling to actually visualize them. Being a farm boy from Pennsylvania, for instance, I thought I understood Jesus' teaching about not turning back after you put your hand to the plow. But it was only after I saw a poor young farmer in Jordan struggling with the same type of one-handed plow his ancestors had used for generations that I began to understand what Jesus was talking about. The Jordanian used his free hand to goad forward his recalcitrant ox. The other hand, the one on the plow handle, could never relax its grip because of the hidden rocks that would in a moment overturn the plow. Looking backward was simply out of the question unless the plowman wanted to land in a tangled heap with his tool and animal. Jesus' hearers understood that logical concept, and I did too—even more clearly after I saw the one-handed plow.

In the same way, I had thought that Jesus' warning to those who would strain out a gnat and swallow a camel was only the juxtaposition of two colorful, unlikely images. I did, that is, until I visited northern India and saw people there straining drinking water with the belief that they were filtering out even bacteria that would compromise their vegetarian beliefs. Others wear masks over their faces hoping to prevent airborne life such as gnats from being accidentally swallowed.

In places as diverse as Egypt, India and Palestine the stories of Bible heroines, like Rebekah, who carried water jars, came alive for me. I saw the women of those countries who, like their forebears for generations, have had the task of drawing and carrying their families' daily water. I watched these modern-day women as they lingered over the fellowship and gossip that is the natural ambiance of the well. Their male counterparts, just as in Bible times, gathered at the city gates for the same social purposes. With new understanding I realized how unusual it must have been for a man to have been doing that exclusively female task of carrying water, and how such a man must have stuck out like a sore thumb in the pre-Passover crowd of Luke 22.

Yes, customs and their symbolic meanings are important, not just to God, but to us who can better understand Him through these emblems. How fortunate we are to have a God who has not only given us laws to help us order our lives, but also stories and symbols and verbal pictures to help us see Him and His qualities more clearly. No amount of dry teaching on the mercy of God can ever be equalled, for instance, by the single, mental picture of the prodigal son's father running to meet his heartsick son. No matter how many synonyms you could find for the word "majestic," they all pale beside the picture we see of Jesus in Revelation 1.

Lewis Sperry Chafer in his book, *Systematic Theology,* lists seven relationships that Christ has with the church that we apprehend through the following symbols: Shepherd and the sheep, Vine and the branches, Cornerstone and stones, High Priest and kingdom of priests, Head and body, Last Adam and new creations, and Bridegroom and bride.

The last relationship, that of Bridegroom and His beloved, is one that is explored in depth in the New Testament, but which can be best comprehended through an understanding of the rich background of marriage customs we read of in the Old Testament. That is the purpose of this book—to explore this marriage relationship of Christ to His church, using some of the marriage customs to help us see that union more clearly. By understanding the union and commitment of Christ and the church, we can better appreciate the union and commitment in the marriage relationship. This is not a marriage manual per se; nor is it intended to inform you how to patch up an ailing marriage. This is no "how to" book; it is rather a "how is" book. Christ did all the work on this marriage. All we have to do is allow ourselves to understand and enjoy it.

Of course, learning about the marriage customs of centuries past is of only limited use if we do not apply that knowledge. As I mentioned before, all biblical symbolism is a filmy and appealing covering through which we can see rock-hard, unchanging truth. You can dress up the concept of love as a compassionate Samaritan or a poor, sacrificing widow or a patient landowner, or you can strip it to its bare essentials on a cross—and it only becomes more lovely. But it becomes useful when we see glimpses of that love in the mirror. And surely God Himself is pleased when He sees it in us, too.

When Jesus spoke of marriage, it was not from firsthand experience, for He Himself never married. He kept Himself for His bride, the church, and for her only. But His concern for earthly marriage covenants is obvious. His very first miracle was not one of saving lives or of healing the hurting. It was one in which He saved a nameless young man and his bride from humiliation at the most important party of their lives—their marriage feast.

Throughout history, God has loved His people with a passionate, single-minded, undeflected devotion. He has caused His Holy Spirit to implant that concept clearly in our minds by having His prophets describe His love for His people in terms that would otherwise be used as love lyrics in a song about earthly relationships. The prophet Isaiah understood this. In Isaiah 54:5 he reminded Israel that their Maker was also their Husband. Later, in chapter 62, he painted the picture of God's rejoicing over the people as being like a bridegroom delighting in his bride.

Jeremiah understood this too. In fact, God told the people through His prophet, "I am your husband." Perhaps nowhere in scripture is this concept more graphically portrayed than in Ezekiel 16. Here Israel is portrayed as a half-breed, unwanted child thrown into an open field at birth, unwashed and squirming in her blood. God not only washed her and cared for her but waited patiently until she was old enough to marry. But she disappointed Him, again and again.

However, God is a persistent Husband. "I will betroth you to Me forever," He declared in Hosea 2:19. His wife might fail, but His love never would.

There are many parallels to this love in the story of Jacob. You will remember how Jacob worked seven long years for the wife of his choice. No sacrifice was too great, just as in the Old Testament God worked tirelessly to "win" Israel. But He, like Jacob, did not get what he bargained for in a wife. So just as Jacob had to go to work again for another wife, so God had set out to "win" the wife who would love Him faithfully, the bride we read about in the New Testament—His church.

So many of Jesus' teachings use illustrations from marriage to prove other points. We read in Matthew 22 of the wedding feast that a man prepared for his son. The wise and foolish virgins, of course, were waiting for a wedding party. Jesus spoke of a bridegroom's guests when He was telling some questioners why His disciples did not fast.

The apostle Paul, however, was the one who most fully explored the imagery of the relationship of Christ, the Bridegroom to His bride, the church. In 2 Corinthians 11:2 he chided his readers by reminding them that he'd promised to present them as a pure bride to their Husband, Christ. And in Romans 7:4 he reminded Christians that we belong to Him.

Ephesians 5 surely crowns Paul's teachings on the extraordinary, husbandly love that Christ has for us. In this chapter, Paul uses the marriage parallel to teach how Christ's love not only demonstrates the nature of His care and concern for us, but actually cleanses us and makes us holy.

And surely this is the most important aspect of His love for us. None of us, upon self-examination, could honestly say that we deserve that kind of love, or that kind of Lover. The fact that our holy Savior would want to unite Himself with us is almost too sacred a thought to bear.

We may not deserve that kind of love, but neither can we resist it. We need it too much. It is reminiscent of the story of the man whose beloved wife became afflicted with a medical problem that affected her jaw and lips. Finally the only recourse found was surgery, but the procedure left her face twisted, her smile crooked. When she was wheeled out of the recovery room, her husband was anxious to set her at ease about her appearance. Carefully and lovingly he leaned over her and pulled his lips to one side to fit hers. Then he gently kissed her.

We, by our sin, have twisted our spiritual smiles. We won't ever be the perfect people we would like to make ourselves. The church won't ever do everything just right. But we are the bride whom Jesus loves. He leans over us each moment of the day, adjusting His lips to ours.

He loves us, and He won't ever stop.

# Chapter 2

## *Marriage and Symbols*

I remember fondly the two-year courtship that Marge and I had so many years ago. I was a senior at Moody Bible Institute, she a junior. We knew, almost from the start, that our courtship was just a prelude to a future life together, one in which we would be used by the Lord as a unit in His service.

Like other young people in love, we tried to spend as much time together as possible. But there were dorm hours and homework and other responsibilities, so we determined to make the most of even our time apart by having simultaneous devotional times, she in her dorm room, I in mine. There we would pray for and about each other, and about our future. One verse that was particularly significant to this new, united life we anticipated was Psalm 34:3, "Oh, magnify the Lord with me. And let us exalt His name together."

In fact, that verse was written on our wedding cake, which was in the shape of a Bible. We wanted the Lord to be a part of our marriage from the very start.

I enjoy the premarital counseling I provide to many young couples. Most of them, like Marge and me, are conscious of God's increasingly important role in their lives. They want everything to be "just right" in His eyes. Many times the bride will ask me for help in planning a wedding ceremony that's "biblical."

### *The Myth of a Biblical Wedding*

It usually comes as a great surprise to these young brides that most of the elements of a traditional "Christian" wedding have their roots not in biblical customs but in those of the ancient Romans. The Roman wedding ceremony became somewhat standardized by the end of the first century, A.D., and according to the author of *Daily Life in Ancient Rome,* Jerome Carcopino, is that "which both in spirit and external form singularly resembles our own, and from which we may be permitted to assume that our own is derived."

A close examination of our Western wedding customs bears out Carcopino's conclusion. Take the month in which most brides are married, for instance. Our month of June is named after Juno, the Roman queen of heaven and goddess of femininity and marriage, whose favor was sought by marriage during "her" month. (Of course, today the ending of the school year in June contributes heavily to the number of June brides, but it has been the most popular wedding month for generations.)

The Roman idea of betrothal was much like our modern engagements. A Roman girl had quite a bit to say about whom she would marry, and when she and her family accepted the proposal of a young man, he would give her gifts that included a ring which he would place on her third finger, left hand. (The Romans believed that there was a vein in this finger which led directly to the heart.) They would join right hands and then kiss. The kiss made the agreement a legal bond, but did not actually obligate them to marry should one or both change their minds.

Later, at the wedding ceremony, the bride and her family would meet the groom and his family at a temple or a sanctuary. She would be dressed with a veil covering the top part of her face and a wreath of flowers on her head. She would wear a coin in her shoe to appease Diana, goddess of chastity, so that she would be able to lose her virginity properly to her husband and thus bear a child.

A religious official would perform a ritual sacrifice and examine the entrails of the animal to make sure that the gods approved of this marriage. Her parents or guardians would hand her over to the care of the bridegroom. Then the couple would exchange mutual vows which ratified their union and made it legally binding. They would then both break a piece from a small wheat cake or biscuit and eat.

Festivities would follow—food, drink, merriment. Later that same day, the wedding party would accompany the groom as he took his new bride to his home. There the bridesmaids would prepare the bride for the nuptial couch, and then modestly retire.

How similar this is to our modern weddings—and how different from the wedding customs we read about in the Bible. Though we will cover each of these aspects in depth later, just the weight of the details is stunning. Consider the following.

A young, Jewish girl of Jesus' time usually had little voice in the selection of her marriage partner. In fact, she might meet him for the first time at her betrothal and then about a year later see him for the second time in her life. During her betrothal she was considered legally married, not just "engaged" and could become "un-engaged" only if her husband divorced her. We have no indication of any rings that signified the betrothal, but there was a ritualistic exchange of money and gifts between the groom, the bride and her parents.

For the bride, the wedding was a spontaneous "surprise" affair conducted not in a place of worship, but outside, at night under a canopy that would remind her of God's promise to Abraham of progeny as numerous as the stars in the sky. She was veiled, but not just her eyes—her entire face was covered. She neither made nor gave any vows but simply listened as the marriage contract was read publicly.

All these things were just a prelude, legally speaking. Their union was not legally complete until some time later when the anxiously waiting guests would hear the announcement that the marriage had been consummated in a nearby room. That was the signal for a wedding "reception" that would last for seven days.

### The "Marriage" of Old and New Customs

It should be obvious by now that the "biblical" wedding ceremony described above is not one that fits our modern ideas of marriage or even of good taste. Some of the elements of such a wedding still exist in a traditional Jewish wedding. Helen Latner,

in a book entitled *Your Jewish Wedding,* describes how modern
Jewish brides still are veiled and marry beneath a canopy or
prayer shawl.

Other elements of a modern Jewish wedding seem to be the
same as in a Christian ceremony, but with vastly different significance. A bride wears white, not to signify virginity but to empha-
size the solemnity of the occasion. In the ceremony, the bride
receives a ring, but it is placed on the index finger of the right
hand, the finger used to point out scripture in the Torah.

Whether they be customs ancient or more modern, they are
passed on from generation to generation and cherished because
they provide a link to the past and to our ancestors. This is especially true of marriage customs because they and the ceremonies
they accompany provide a line of demarcation in our individual
lives, a way of accounting change, a before-and-after bookmark
in our personal histories.

Such symbols are important, not only to help us remember
vows and events, but also because of what they signify. Though it is
admirable to want to have a "biblical" wedding, I counsel young
brides simply to choose whatever symbols they want in their weddings. The exchange of vows is not found in the Bible, but who
among us would feel married without them? A "unity candle" has
no relation to the oil lamps of the virgins in the wedding parties of
Jesus' times, yet it can concretely picture for the wedding guests
the joining of two family lines into one. King Tut placed one of
his sandals on the foot of his wife, signifying unity and oneness
in marriage.

These and other customs of our times are not only acceptable to God, I feel, but are actually pleasing to Him as long as
they portray the holiness, permanency and joy of the marriage
covenant.

Both practices or customs as well as physical objects serve
as symbols in our lives. They have meaning far beyond their own
presence or being. A ring, for instance, may evoke memories of
the excitement of choosing it with one's mate, but even the form
of it is meant to signify something greater to anyone who sees it
on the hand: an unending circle that symbolizes thoughts of unending love. Diamonds in our culture represent an outlay of a

considerable amount of money (and thus commitment) as well as
telling us something by their clarity, brilliance and durability.

It is not necessary for any of the wedding symbols we enjoy
to have any basis in Scripture as long as they do not violate its
spirit. The same God who blessed the marriage canopy of the
young, Jewish bride will surely embrace the altars and spires or
judges' chambers or backyard trellises of any young couple who
commit themselves to Him and to each other.

### Marriage as a Symbol in the Old Testament

We can see the "evolution," so to speak, of marriage as a symbol
as we read the Bible chronologically. You will recall that God
gave Eve to Adam without ceremony, simply stating that it was
not good for him to be alone. The "point" of their wedding was
not vows, like the Roman wedding, nor consummation, like Jewish weddings. It was the unadorned filling of a need.

We see this theme of companionship satisfied and progeny promised throughout the book of Genesis—godly men like
Abraham seeking wives from among their own people, comforted
like Isaac, surrounded by children and grandchildren like Jacob
in Egypt. By the time of the writing of Proverbs 31, the picture
emerges of a wife whose multifaceted talents bring honor to her
husband and joy to her children. The husband of Psalm 128, too,
was prosperous, happy, blessed.

Up until this time in Scripture, marriage seemed to stand
for nothing more than itself: the joining together of people for
their mutual benefit and for the furtherance of the race.

By the time of the prophet Hosea in the eighth century
B.C., however, marriage in prophetic writing became a symbol of
something beyond that of a man-woman relationship. The betrothal ceremony took on new significance when God announced
that He would treat the nation of Israel collectively as His own
fiancée (Hosea 2:19–20).

Two centuries later in the period of the Exile, Ezekiel em-
phasized this espousal by telling the Jews that God had sworn
loyalty to them, entering into a covenant as enduring as that of
marriage (Ezekiel 16:8).

The Old Testament pages close with the book of Malachi and its transmittal of God's flat statement: "I hate divorce." In Jewish culture, the long-past days of polygamy and concubinage were gone. Monogamy had become the only acceptable marriage state, and Malachi warned sternly about the danger of putting away a Jewish wife in order to marry a foreign woman.

Though the teachings on divorce are unmistakably plain, their meaning was intended to stretch far beyond man-woman relationships. When God warned against the putting away of the wife of one's youth, He was not speaking only of marriage. Here, in a way not found anywhere else in Scripture, God spoke of the relationship between Himself and His beloved Israel as a marriage wherein Israel was the husband, and He the cast-off wife.

Surely the shocking image of the God of the universe becoming so familiar that He would be dumped in favor of a newer, more exciting mate was an image that must have haunted God's people during the five long centuries of silence from the brass-hard heavens before the birth of Jesus.

## A New Testament Symbol of Marriage

How frustrating that divine muteness must have been. Not only was there no direction from heaven as in the old days, the whole nation of Israel was divided and scattered and passed from conquering power to conquering power like a worn-out toy from child to child. Any time they were freed, it was only freedom to be dominated by another hateful, foreign ruler.

The arrogant statement of the Jews in John 8:33 who told Jesus, "We are Abraham's descendants, and have never been in bondage to anyone," must have seemed pitiful in its equivocation, even to the hardened hearts of its speakers. The nation of Israel, the once-proud bride-to-be of God, was at best an indentured servant with no visible hope of release.

By refusing to acknowledge their own condition of slavery, the Jews also could not recognize the need to be set free. They did not realize that their Liberator was right there, before them.

How far was He willing to go to free them? Their slavery brings to mind the situation found in Exodus 21. There we read of the devotion of a husband who after working for seven years would find himself free to leave his servitude. If such a man would find himself more bound by his love for his wife than for a life of freedom, the servant could go before an authority and renounce his freedom. Then he could go with his master and allow his master to pierce his ear with an awl, driving it through that tender tissue into a doorpost.

Thus a husband could give up, permanently, his rights as a free man so that he could share the rest of his life with his wife whom he loved more than his own liberty.

Jesus was that husband. He gladly took on the prison of earthlife, the confines of a physical body—He who as God is as limitless as the universe He created. In Hebrews 10:5–7, He said:

> Sacrifice and offering You did not desire,
>     but a body You have prepared for Me.
> In burnt offerings and sacrifices for sin
>     You had no pleasure.
> Then I said, "Behold, I have come—In the volume of the Book
>     it is written of Me—
> to do Your will, O God."

This passage is a quote from Psalm 40:6–8. The Hebrew translation of the phrase, "a body You have prepared for me," is translated in the New International Version as, "my ears you have pierced."

Perhaps our image of Christ needs to be revised somewhat. Oh, we remember the wounds on His hands and feet. We recall with a shudder the gaping place in His side where a man's hand would fit. The lash marks on His back and shoulders, the scraped places on His knees and elbows where He fell, the wounds in His forehead where the crown of thorns was forced on—these have been burned into our consciousness all our lives.

Add to these, though, the invisible wounds of a Husband, one with tiny scars on His earlobes, who thought this all out ahead of time, who knows that all these lesions represent lifelong love, and who does not ever regret it.

# Chapter 3

## *The Purpose of Marriage*

The crescendo of the angels' voices must have echoed throughout eternity's vast vacuum. Like a million radio transmitters all emitting song, they were heard by only one Receiver, the only Being besides themselves then in existence: their Creator. He, the Prototype of all power, stood poised on the brink of the execution of His completed plan.

Nothing would ever be the same.

With His spoken word and the resultant flash of blinding light, history began. The convulsions of earth and heaven—celestial bodies majestic in their appointed places, fleeing seas and thrust-up dry land, lushness and greenery, then the miracle of life-breath in myriad creatures—each followed another in an orderly parade.

In a final, intoxicating spasm of creativity, the dust of this new earth was kneaded and sculpted and breathed upon. There before Him was His own image, staring back at Him with trusting child-eyes.

Before the man himself knew it, God saw his aloneness. With the rib that would forever be a reminder of his incompleteness, God completed Adam. The Being who throughout eternity had been self-sufficient began His relationship with mankind with an assertion that would forever mark us both: aloneness is not good. It is for this reason that "God setteth the solitary in families" (Psalm 68:6 KJV).

With this admission, the same God who saw a deficit in man revealed in Himself the same yearning. From that point on,

He would create a pattern whereby He would continue to show Himself to His creation, making Himself vulnerable, repeating His openness, craving companionship and communication from the dust-based products of His hand.

This great God let Himself be seen striding purposefully through the mists of history, stopping here and there to let Himself be understood by the childlike minds of His people. And soon they began to see themselves as an entity with a special relationship with Him.

Through Abraham, He announced His engagement to this special, fledgling people. He fell in love with her in her infancy. He watched over her as she left her home to go to Egypt. He sought her—and found her—and brought her home.

On Mount Sinai, He even prepared a prenuptial agreement. And from that point on through the Old Testament, we see Him doggedly pursuing His fickle fiancée, Israel, as she cavorted and flirted with any other lover who would look her way.

Why? Why would the God of eternity love a people so much? This vision of a vulnerable God who can love us, and even reach out for us, startles us. The realization that His love can have no end and no divorce clause forever changes anyone who grasps its import.

God's love affair with His people is a theme-thread that is woven tightly and unmistakably through the writings of the Old and New Testaments. Only to modern people unfamiliar with scripture is the idea of a Husband-God, an Eternal Spouse, strange. Its importance to the Jewish nation historically can't be overestimated.

Israel was a passionate people who not unwittingly acted out prophecy that often decreed their own doom; they looked at the Law as both jailer and liberator; but they tried repeatedly to replicate in their own lives the patterns they saw in Scripture. If aloneness was not good, they reasoned, they should all marry.

Indeed, the Jews of Jesus' day believed that the only reason a Jewish man could give for refusal to marry was that he had made a prior commitment to devote his life to the study of the Law. Further, members of the Sanhedrin (the supreme council of the Jewish people) were actually required to be married men, because such were believed to be more merciful.

By the time a young man had reached the age of eighteen, he was expected to have made this momentous decision. Josephus noted that a man's prospective wife must be a virgin of good parentage—not a slave nor a prostitute—nor the former wife of any other. In fact, the expectations and strictures put on these young men were so much a part of the fabric of Jewish life that men who did not marry—like Jesus, for instance, and John the Baptist—were regarded at best as oddities and at worst as fanatics. And then, a few decades later, that rebel Paul suggested that some believers during times of persecution would be better off if they never married! Truly this Christianity was a revolutionary way of thinking.

For in this new covenant, God's Son promised to take His people as His bride, once and for all. True to the Jewish way of thinking, our betrothal is as binding and as final as our inevitable marriage. We, His church, live separated from Him during this long engagement. But we belong to each other.

The mystery of all this, of course, is not in its consummation, but in our own worthiness. The wonder is in the fact that Christ not only died for us—we can grasp that one-time act—but that He wants to live with us forever.

### *Companionship—One Purpose for Marriage*

We stand in our twentieth-century, culture-bound confines and speculate about the reasons those ancient people had for marrying, and we sometimes forget they were motivated by the human desires common to all men. Again the voice of God echoes to us from Eden's gate: For most of us, it is not good to be alone.

Philosophers of all creeds have repeated this truth. Plato, the Greek sage, theorized that mankind came originally in a "double package," twice what we are now. Because of mankind's arrogance, he said, the gods cut each person in half, and true happiness could only be realized when the two halves found each other and were reunited. Many people have ached with the secret suspicion that Plato was right: Although we might be happy and productive with any number of potential marriage partners, we could only be complete with that one special person.

That yearning need for completion, once it is satisfied, becomes a powerful, giving force that energizes a relationship. This is reflected in the lovely Hebrew word for marriage, *kiddushin.* Barclay says that this word refers to a holiness or consecration—sanctification—instead of a feeling of satiety. The purity of total surrender to one's beloved becomes not only the glue that holds a relationship together but a badge of its validity.

Perhaps it was an appeal to this Hebrew word which was in the mind of Paul when he said that marriage could "sanctify" even an unbelieving mate.

If that is true, then how much more it must consecrate believers in our relationship with God! For we, even more than the unsaved, are conscious of our great sinfulness, our fallen nature, and we must strain to comprehend why the God of the universe would want companionship with us. Ephesians 5 teaches us of this "profound mystery"—that God, through Christ, has chosen the church as His bride. He desires a holy relationship with us, an intimacy like that of marriage.

And so we bumble pell-mell into trying to spend time with Him (for is that not, we reason, the meaning of companionship?). But after we've failed at our Bible-reading schedules and benevolence meetings, and passed up our private prayer time for other pursuits, we find that these are just means to an end. Our eternal Husband does not want our programs, He wants us.

Nor is His reaching out for us selfish. Christ initiated this relationship with us knowing that He would always be the sacrificing one, and we would always be the recipients of His bounty. Few of us would enter into a marriage with the Calvary mindset: resolved always to be the giver in our relationship, and expecting little or nothing of value to ourselves in return. What He wants, as the invitations used to read, is "the pleasure of our company."

### *Marriage—Blessing and Bridle on our Desires*

Earthly marriage is often predicated upon sexual need, and sometimes solely on it, as attested to by the high divorce rate we have in this country. But the magical attraction between male and female is real, and even valid in God's eyes. Though it was not usually the motivation for marriage in Jewish culture (but rather an expected outgrowth of marriage), we still see glimpses of it in the Old Testament: in the love-at-first-sight meeting of Isaac and Rebekah; in the yearning of Jacob for Rachael; in Boaz who was riveted to the young Moabitess gleaning in his field; and of course in the Song of Solomon.

Throughout the ages, we have yearned for the ideal; for that consummation of personalities that is somehow finalized in the act of sex. We are grateful for the lack of embarrassment that the Bible evinces in its treatment of this most basic of human desires.

The union of two, in a way that mathematics is powerless to explain, makes the unit so formed much stronger than the mere sum of both. The ancient Jews assumed that a married man even by himself would be much more productive than a willfully unmarried counterpart. And even across the millennia that separate us, we understand this fact.

When we unite ourselves with Christ, we can as individuals feel the empowering result of having been chosen by Him. The incomprehensible, divine urges that motivate Him are beyond our understanding, so we abandon analysis and content ourselves with revelling in that love, reflecting it like the sparkle of an engagement ring.

Just as marriage is thus a liberator of all our pent-up desires, it serves also as a bridle for them. In the earthly sense, this satisfaction acts as a preventive to unfaithfulness. Over and over marriage is commended in the Bible as a way to prevent immorality: "Nevertheless, to avoid fornication, let every man have his own wife, and let every woman have her own husband" (1 Corinthians 7:2 KJV).

So, too, our devotion to Christ will automatically preclude relationships with other people or other things that would ultimately harm us. When you are truly in love, no other person can do more than just momentarily catch your eye. We don't become immune to outside attractions, we just don't succumb to them.

### Reproduction—Numbers and Names

For the Jews, children were no mere by-product of marriage; in many cases, they were a primary purpose for marriage. The Genesis admonition to "multiply and replenish the earth" (Genesis 1:28 KJV) historically has been taken so seriously by Jews that even some modern-day Jews throw wheat (sometimes with coins mixed in) at weddings to signify the blessings of children on that union.

Our home was blessed with our first child two years after our marriage. We thought of him, and later our other children, as a loan from God, just as Hannah regarded Samuel. The time we spent teaching our children God's laws and their underlying principles was for us an investment, both in our spiritual welfare as well as in their lives. And we have never regretted a moment so spent.

Naturally, we wanted to give them the best we could, and the sacrifices we made for them were a joy. But I have often been amazed to consider how different this thinking is from the way Old Testament people thought of children. Surely, they loved their children and were happy to supply their needs. But as 2 Corinthians 12:14 shows, the custom in those days was for the children to save up in order to supply their aging parents' needs. Again, how revolutionary Paul was—and how much he has taught us—in his willingness to break with old customs and show us how to serve each other.

The "utilitarian" valuation of children was reflected in the way the Israelites counted their children. Many times in the Old Testament we read of how many sons a certain person had. Sometimes daughters were not even mentioned. Why was this? Well, sons could work in the fields and take over the family trade when the father died, perpetuating both his vocation and his name. Daughters, on the other hand, were useful workers, but only temporary, for when they married, they became part of someone else's family. I have been aware of this thinking even today and heard many an Arab father of five offspring say, "I have three children, and two girls," meaning he has three sons and two daughters.

For an ancient Israelite woman, childbearing was a social and psychological necessity ("Give me children or I will die!" cried Rachael). She, along with Sarah, Hannah and others, felt incomplete as a woman until she had children. Tamar in Genesis 38 was the first woman in the Bible who actually demanded her "right" to have children under the levirate system that guaranteed even a widow a chance at motherhood. Other women, such as the daughters of Lot, took their desire to have children so seriously that they went to even more extreme lengths (in this case, those daughters slept with their drunken father Lot in order to conceive). While neither the Scriptures nor I condone such actions, they do point out this unmistakable fact: having children was not optional to the ancient Jew.

It is not stretching the analogy to say that our fruitfulness in our relationship with Christ can do all the things that having children did for an Israelite marriage. We "replenish" the kingdom of God on earth in several ways. First, we teach our own physical offspring—our sons and daughters—to be godly people so that they can continue the kingdom-building that has wearied our shoulders and calloused our hands.

Secondly, we spiritually reproduce ourselves each time we bring someone to Christ. This reproduction, though, is not limited by health or childbearing years or house size or finances, but only by our willingness. Just as we carefully consider the way an infant will affect our lives, so must we count the cost of nurturing a newborn soul in the kingdom. It is not a question of a few spiritual meals and good times; it is a process of pain and growth and lifelong commitment.

By helping people be converted to Christ, we mirror another purpose that Israelites had in marriage: that of carrying on the name of the father. We are reminded of the importance of this in reading the story of the wise woman of Tekoa in 2 Samuel 14. This woman, you will recall, went before King David ostensibly to plead for the life of her only remaining son, who had killed his brother. This widow appealed to David on the basis of the fact that if this remaining son were executed, her dead husband would have no one to carry on his name.

Her appeal, you will also recall, was remarkably effective.
Later, we ache for Absalom, who erected a large pillar in the King's
Valley in his own memory—the pitiful actions of a man who real-
ized that he had no son to carry on his name. Again and again the
Scriptures echo the sentiment that a father with no offspring was
disgraced.

It is not difficult to see a spiritual parallel. We disgrace our
heavenly Father if we do not reproduce ourselves. We know from
New Testament teachings that we are not all required to marry
and have physical children, but none of us is exempt from sharing
the message with others. True, not all can preach or write, but all
must either by life or by lips show the results of redemption to
those around us.

We fool ourselves, perhaps, but not the world if we think
that our union with Christ can be without fruit. The world knows
from observing nature that you cannot have two fertile partners
and an intimate relationship without some eventual result! If our
relationship to Christ is not bearing fruit, then one partner is
withholding or sterile or both.

Christ is none of these. He is our loving, giving partner. It is
not because we are righteous that He loves us. It is not because we
"believe"—indeed, He loved us long before.

Sure, we "consent" to this relationship with Him, and con-
gratulate ourselves on what a lucky catch we've made—a lifelong
partner who would (and did!) die for us.

What luck? No—
What love!

# Chapter 4

## *The Selection of the Bride*

The image, the memory imbedded in the mind of each of us, stays with us throughout our lives: that time in our childhood or youth when we were not chosen.

It may have been for the spelling bee, or for the play. But for most of us, the most common experience involved the sandlot ball team. As we watched helplessly, others around us walked away, into a belonging that, with its inaccessibility, became increasingly more desirable. We may have drawn circles in the dirt with a foot, desperately trying to pretend ignorance of the situation, or we may have defiantly announced that we did not care. Many of us found to our panic that we were suddenly overcome by the hot, bitter tears we could not hold back.

Nor was the aftermath any easier to bear: being reluctantly placed in the outfield because we were "left over" at the end of the side-choosing process, the little-suppressed groans of our more able teammates, the sick feeling of not being welcome.

Even as adults, being passed over for a promotion or snubbed by an acquaintance brings back to us in a rush those childhood feelings, that we are only being endured, never chosen. No matter how we resist it, we transport ourselves to a place where nothing else but the hurting exists, and we are alone with our pain.

Nothing in this life takes the place of the feeling we have when someone by words or actions says: "I choose you." When someone makes a deliberate decision to include us, we are vindicated as human beings, given worth and imputed value.

Nowhere else is this so necessary as in a marriage relationship, for that is where we most wish to be intimately known and accepted for what we are. In our twentieth-century culture, this acceptance is often conditional upon appearance or appeal or assets; and choices of a marriage partner sometimes involve all these. But the idea of selecting one's own mate is a new one, relatively speaking, and is, in certain parts of the world, as yet unknown.

Not long ago I spent eight days in Nagpur, India. I had many appointments, so I hired a "cab" driver, someone who would transport me in a three-wheeled motorized rickshaw. My driver looked to be about twenty-one, and we became friends during the time we spent together. I was sorry, one night, when he told me that the next day would be his last to be my driver because he was getting married.

"How long have you two been going together?" I asked. He seemed amused at my question.

"Well, Mr. Greenwood," he answered, "I have never met my bride-to-be. My parents arranged the wedding when we were both much younger." He was beaming as he told me of this and of the trust he had in his parents' choice.

"But do you think you will be happy with this young woman?"

"Oh, yes!" he replied. "My parents love me so much that they would only choose the best for me. She will be my equal, socially and economically. No, we will have few problems, because she was selected very carefully. My parents would do anything to prevent my being hurt by a bad marriage."

He continued as I nodded, unable to respond. "And I am committed to this marriage. It will last, and it will be good for both her family, and for mine, as well as for our new life together."

It is only experiences like this, and contact with Jewish culture, through plays like *Fiddler on the Roof,* that we are reminded that love has not always preceded marriage. Indeed, when we look for love matches in the Bible, they are few—Jacob and Rachael, Samson and his Philistine bride, Ruth and Boaz, David and Michal, the lovers in Song of Solomon.

The basis for the choice of a wife in Bible times was more dependent on suitability than attraction. We hear another

Eden-echo in God's studied intention to provide a wife for His new man, one who would be a help "meet," or suitable, for him.

"Forty days before a child is formed," the rabbinical tradition goes, "a heavenly voice proclaims its mate." A young man in the apocryphal book of Tobit was told of his bride, "she was prepared for thee from the beginning." And in the book of Proverbs we read that "a prudent wife is from the Lord." To the Jewish mind, the implications were unmistakable: the selection process of marriage began not on earth but in the mind of God Himself.

## The Choosing of a Wife

Prudent as they were, the ancient Jews were loathe to leave such important decisions to anything as risky as human emotion. Throughout scripture, the father specifically was given the task of selecting a bride for his son. Many times this was done as a result of the father's observation of a young woman, but more often it was done on the basis of the suitability of the girl's family—the compatibility of her social class and economic status, as well as the family's reputation and standing in the community. Many times it was the groom's father who approached the bride's family with the marriage offer, but just as Abraham sent a trusted servant to choose a wife for Isaac, a marriage broker or messenger was often employed. Nonetheless, the father's opinion was final.

If a young man had no father, the mother was allowed to select his future bride for him. Or, a trusted friend of the family might perform this function as Jehoida in 2 Chronicles chose wives for Joash.

The examples in scripture of young men who chose their own wives seem almost always tinged with sorrow. Isaac and Rebekah grieved all their lives for their restless son Esau's rash choice of two Hittite women for his wives. We can feel Jacob's bitter disappointment when weak-eyed Leah was substituted in the darkness of his marriage bed for his beloved Rachael. We ache for the lovesick Shechem who begged his father to negotiate for the lovely young Dinah. And Samson's urgent "get her for me" in regard to the Philistine beauty who caught his eye is just the opening statement in a tragic story of unfulfilled love, betrayal and eventual death.

Sometimes a wife was chosen for a young man as a result of a great feat he might perform. In this case the woman was a reward for the young man's valor, whether he took her as booty in a war or earned her as David did Michal by his defeat of the Philistine forces. Forever after, such a wife would be a reminder of his strength, a visible badge of victory.

Often it was a king who awarded such a wife, and that sovereign's ability to make choices for his subjects was absolute. After David "earned" Michal, for instance, Saul had the power to give her to another man. Even Tamar, as she was being raped by her half-brother Amnon, tried to reason with him by telling him that their father the king could authorize this incestuous union.

Only rarely did the bride of Old Testament times have any say in the choice of her husband. But there are a few notable exceptions. The daughters of Zelophehad in Numbers 36 were allowed to choose their own husbands as long as they were from within their own tribe to keep the land inheritance of their father within his own clan instead of having it pass with their marriages to one of the other tribes. Their gracious God allowed them to take the aggressive role in choosing their own mates.

Rebekah stands out in Bible history as an example of a woman who apparently was held in very high regard, for when the arrangements were made for her marriage to Isaac, she was actually consulted about when she would leave her family to go to him. Such consultation of the bride-to-be, though, was apparently a rare thing in those days.

In only one other situation were women given the prerogative of choosing their own husbands. In those days before Social Security and widows' benefits, a woman whose husband died was at the mercy of a cruel economic system. If she had no children to help her, she was doubly disadvantaged. Our gracious God provided for this eventuality through a system we know as levirate marriage. Under this system, a childless widow could go to any of her deceased husband's brothers and request that he marry her and take care of her. If he had no brothers, a near relative would do. In the case of Ruth, her mother-in-law Naomi advised her to approach Boaz, a relative of her deceased husband, and indicate this choice of him by uncovering his feet while he slept. He in turn indicated his acceptance by covering her with his garment.

By law, a man was required not only to take such a close relative's widow into his household, but to live conjugally with her. A son born from that union bore the name of the deceased so that his family line would not become extinct. Because of this practice of levirate marriage, it is easy for us to understand why the men of a family would take a very close look at any young woman that a brother of theirs might think of marrying. It was not unlikely that this woman might someday be married to one of them.

### Factors Influencing the Choice of a Bride

Most young women became betrothed between the ages of twelve and fifteen. Even Mary, Christ's mother, was probably not older than fifteen. We may be surprised by this, but we must remember that the greatest heroine of love of our Anglo-Saxon culture was the young girl Juliet who was about that same age when she fell in love with Romeo.

At such a tender age, a young Jewish girl had probably led such a sheltered existence that she had done little to distinguish herself, good or bad. Only in rare cases (hard-working Rebekah is an example) were a girl's individual traits the primary consideration that a father or marriage-broker took into account when choosing her. Of greater importance were her family's reputation and standing in the community.

Most important, the girl had to be of Jewish parentage. We are amazed when we see the number of times in the Old Testament that God demanded that His people marry only within their own race. Sometimes this required the marriage of a near relative, as in the case of Abram and Sarai, and Isaac and Rebekah. Two factors must be considered as we admit the justice of such a practice.

First of all, incest as we would today define it did not in pre-Mosaic times carry the stigma it now has. Arthur Custance in his book *Time and Eternity* has done a marvelous scientific study. In it he shows how early in the history of the world, God's people could marry close family members and escape the birth defects and genetic problems that may accompany such a union today. Why? Because the gene pool was as yet unpolluted.

Secondly, the Bible points us again and again to examples of people like Solomon who married outside their race, outside their culture, and ultimately, outside their God.

It was also proper for a family to seek a bride who was from the same socioeconomic status as the son. F. Scott Fitzgerald was not the first to say that "poor boys should not think to marry rich girls." David had first voiced that thought thousands of years before (1 Samuel 18:18, 23). Part of this was because, as we shall see, a poor man could not afford the *mohar* or bride-price (discussed in chapter six) that a bride of high position would expect.

Many times the choice of a bride was made not behind closed tent doors but at the site of a village well. Indeed, this was the gathering place for all the women of the town, the nearest equivalent to a women's social club that ancient Israel had to offer. Here they came in the cool of the day to draw the life-sustaining water, to meet friends, to exchange the news of the day. Here, too, a bride-chooser could come and observe the women. Abraham's servant, Jacob and Moses all found brides at a well.

Many such a go-between was spared unnecessary (and perhaps embarrassing) questions about a young girl's social position, for only the daughters of wealthy families carried brass water pots. The rest bore clay jars with little or no decoration.

Surely the choosing of a bride would have taken much of the time and energy of parents in those days, for their choice would affect not only their son but the family name they so treasured. We can imagine the long conversations in Judean evenings between the parents, the urgent, whispered directives to the servant or friend who acted as go-between, the agonizing waiting during negotiations. This choice would forever mark the lives of all involved.

### God's Choice of a Bride

The parallels between the bride-selection process in those ancient days, and our personal relationship with Christ is a rich and fertile field that yields greater harvests each time we enter it. We are awed by the realization that we were chosen by God as a suitable helper for our Lord.

No matter how frequent or how painful our past experiences with rejection were, we are bolstered by this present fact: we have been chosen. We were not the leftovers, but God's first choice. Like the young man in Nagpur, India, we know our Parent well. We know that the mate He chose for His Son was the right one. We trust His judgment and respect His assessment. We do, that is, until we consider who He chose. He chose me and you. And we know ourselves too well to be comfortable with this idea. If He is all-knowing, why did He choose us?

Like the young women of Bible times, we know of a certainty that we were ignorant of the choosing while it was in process. The plans for our betrothal to Christ were made long ago, even before the founding of this world.

He must have had His eye on us for a long time. We are conscious of the fact that He was planning our future life while we were spiritual infants. He waited patiently as we matured, during that long and painful time of adolescence, even while we flirted with the world.

And then, He sent a matchmaker. It may have been a friend or a parent who introduced us to Christ. But it was someone who knew us and knew Jesus and knew He was "just perfect" for us. And our union ever since has been enriching and satisfying, the joy of our lives.

Our Heavenly Father went through a similar process with that marvelous, corporate entity we know as the church. Long ago, He deliberately chose a people, the nation of Israel. He made it clear from the start that it was a love match that had nothing to do with the social standing, or even the worthiness of the people. "The Lord did not set His love on you nor choose you because you were more in number than other people, for you were the least of all peoples," Moses told them. "But [it was] because the Lord loves you . . ." (Deuteronomy 7:7–8a).

Romans 9 shows us that we who believe are children of the promise, no matter what our ancestry. We are heirs to all the wonderful things those ancient people were promised. God has set His affection on us, too, and He loves us as well. The proof of this is in the fact that this ultimate "Jewish" Father chose us to be the bride for His only son. This marriage must work for

His name to be carried on. God hates divorce, and there is no backup plan.

His betrothed, the church, is perfect. No, we didn't come to Him that way. We were "yet sinners." We, like the pitiful, abandoned infant of Ezekiel 16, were thrown out into an open field at birth, despised by all about us except for the One who passed by and saw us there, kicking about in our blood, and who said to us, "Live!"

It was that gift of life itself that began His people's relationship with Him. While we grew and matured, He was watching, communicating with His Father about us, charting our development. Then when we became old enough for love, as Ezekiel put it, He announced His choice of us, to be His church, to be His bride.

Of course, He had a friend to help Him, that near relative to serve as go-between and best man. He was that fearless herald of the kingdom, John the Baptist. "I have been sent before him," John joyfully shared with his own disciples (John 3:28).

But, we protest, we aren't suitable prospects for such a union with Jesus. We could never claim to be of the same race as He. We certainly could never be on the same "economic" level as the Owner of all things. And what of our heritage of sin and rebellion?

It would be a romantic thought to believe that for us, His bride, Jesus was willing to break all the rules and to ignore all the practices we see in Old Testament scripture when He selected His own bride. But Jesus never was a law-breaker or a rebel. He always fulfilled the Law. So instead of putting aside these old ways, or changing them, He simply changed us.

We, who with hopelessly jumbled genealogies could never prove Jewish ancestry, would be beyond even the dream of marrying the Nazarene. But those who were excluded from citizenship, He made part of His own people. He disregarded the ignominy of our parentage and overlooked our "family" reputation.

He chose us.

Carrying only the shoddiest of clay pots that marked us as destitute, we came to the well of our lives looking for water. We came away refreshed and betrothed to a Husband who owns the cattle on a thousand hills and who was willing to pay the highest bride-price of all: His own life.

# Chapter 5

## *The Betrothal*

A Jewish bride-to-be must have felt relatively powerless over the process of being chosen as a wife. As she walked with her companions daily to the village well, or as she and her mother performed the intimate monthly ritual of laundering her menstrual cloths in a nearby stream, she must have taken those opportunities to ask married women the questions that must have burned through her young-girl heart.

As the visits between her home and that of her admirer increased, her anticipation and curiosity must have mounted. Any of us who have ever experienced a life-passage such as the first day of college away from home, or the death of a loved one, or marriage, can certainly remember that feeling of unreality which accompanies such an event. No matter how we may have planned (or tried to prepare for) such things, the world suddenly becomes disjointed; we often feel we are detached observers of our own lives; and reality is only contacted through physical means: a letter from home, a ring on the finger, the touching of a loved one's face in a casket.

Surely she must have wondered sometimes if the flurry of activity that accompanied the matchmaker's visits, the talk of negotiations, and the sidelong glances were all just her imagination—signs of something too good to be true. But finally, usually unexpectedly, the day came when she was called from her chambers and asked to become a participant in this process. For her, the reality of her coming marriage would be realized through three concrete things: a cup, a contract and the construction of a bridal chamber.

## *The Cup*

The Old Testament Jews had several ways in which they signified or ratified an agreement. God, for instance, sealed His covenant with Abram by passing between the halves of sacrificial animals, a practice that became a customary way of sealing such contracts. In negotiating to take Ruth as his wife, Boaz finalized the arrangements by giving his sandal to her former kinsman-redeemer.

The marriage covenant, though, was most often sealed with a cup of wine. After the negotiations over the bride-price (which will be dealt with in the coming chapter) were settled, there must have been a feeling of relief in the Judean home where the bridegroom had come to arrange for his life-partner. In that atmosphere of dissolving tensions and new fellowship, the bride's parents and the bridegroom would introduce a new element—the bride herself.

She who had been the object of all these frenetic maneuverings was often kept largely ignorant of them until the moment she was called from her bedroom for perhaps her first sight of the man with whom she would share the rest of her life. Being in his presence, in the same room with him, must have been exhilarating, for this, combined with the brimming cup of wine from which they would drink, would provide the touchstone of reality in what must have seemed to her to be a dream.

That cup of wine signified three things. First of all, it was the finalizing element in the contract of marriage that the bridegroom had negotiated with the girl's parents. Like a signature on a legal document, it symbolized the exchange of three elements of great value: money, promises and bachelor freedom the bridegroom was willing to sacrifice to purchase this treasure, his future wife.

It was also a toast, a salute of tribute to this young woman, for no matter how many compliments she had heretofore received in her life, none could compare with this fact: someone wanted her.

Finally, the girl's acceptance of the cup meant that she accepted the young man himself to be her future husband. As she looked shyly into his eyes, tasting the richness of the wine, she completed this covenant. She must be willing, because marriage, like wine, had its inherent dangers. It could be sweet, it could be intoxicating, it could make the heart glad or damn their souls. The secret, she would doubtless discover, would not be in the wine itself nor in the marriage contract itself: but in their attitude toward each other.

### The Contract

We in the twentieth-century Western world tend to think of that period of time after a man asks a woman to marry him until the marriage is actually finalized as being a trial period, a time in which both parties seriously evaluate their coming commitments. During this time, either the man or the woman can, for even a whim, break off the relationship with relatively few legal or emotional repercussions.

However, this was not the case in Bible times. When a young man paid the bride-price and sealed that contract (the "tenaim") with the cup, he actually acquired legal possession of her, though he might not take physical possession of her until the marriage ceremony. For all intents and purposes, she became his legal wife at the moment of betrothal.

The Greek word that describes a betrothed woman is often translated "espoused," a word that carries within it the idea of the woman already being a "spouse." Such a woman was referred to as a wife even before the marriage was consummated (Deuteronomy 20:7, 28:30).

There are many examples in scripture of women who were referred to as wives of the men to whom we would say they were merely engaged. Jacob, for example, demanded that Laban give him Rachael—"my wife"—after he had paid the bride-price of seven years of labor for her (Genesis 29:21). David also asked Ish-Bosheth to send his betrothed, Michal, to him, calling her "wife" even though they were not married—in fact, Michal had been given in marriage to Paltiel son of Laish (2 Samuel 3:14–15).

Of course, the most familiar story that illustrates the binding nature of a betrothal is found in Matthew chapter 1, where we read of how Joseph had decided to terminate his betrothal to the pregnant Mary—not by "breaking their engagement," but by a legal procedure of divorce (v. 19).

Divorce was one of only two ways that a betrothal could be terminated. Genesis 34 and Deuteronomy 22 both illustrate that a woman's sexual infidelity, except in cases of rape, during the betrothal period was treated as adultery with the same penalties.

It appears that Palestinian and Babylonian Jews stringently enforced the binding concept of the betrothal. Among the Alexandrian Jews, however, there was more flexibility. The Greco-Egyptian influence allowed them to treat this betrothal time more as we do, as a conditional engagement more than the first stage of marriage. But this way of thinking was the exception to an otherwise inviolate rule in Jewish culture.

Aside from divorce, the only other way out of a betrothal was the death of one of the parties involved. Barclay in his *Daily Study Bible* noted that if a betrothed man died, the young woman he was to have married was referred to, according to Jewish law, as "a virgin who is a widow," for she became his wife when she was betrothed to him.

So, therefore, when a young Jewish girl drank from that betrothal cup, she said, in effect, "until death do us part."

### The Construction of the Bridal Chamber

The third concrete element that would symbolize the coming marriage was the bridal chamber that the young man would build for his wife. Zola Levitt, a Hebrew-Christian writer, details how such a young man would hurry home from the betrothal ceremony and immediately begin work on the special place where he and his bride would honeymoon. Sometimes he would simply decorate a room in his father's house, but more often he would construct a small, separate building on his father's property.

Into this "little mansion" he would pour all his creative efforts for the coming months, making it as luxurious as he could afford, as beautiful as his imagination would allow. There he would stockpile the special provisions they would eat during the seven days they would be together in there, alone.

Surely the friends of the betrothed girl would bring her news of how the construction process was proceeding, and if he lived nearby, the sounds of hammering and sawing must have daily confirmed his love for her. This building process continued usually for nearly a year, and toward the end of this time tensions must have run high, for the chamber was only complete when the groom's father declared it complete. The father's relative detachment from the emotions the young man must have felt kept him from letting this groom throw up a slipshod structure in his haste to claim his wife.

While her husband worked tirelessly on the bridal chamber, the betrothed young woman had her own preparations to make. Some of those preparations were of a physical nature. Perhaps she experimented with "beauty treatments" like young Esther did before her marriage (Esther 2:12). Doubtless her curiosity about her duties as wife and homemaker increased, and such things as laundry and cooking took on new meaning.

Clothing, especially, became very important to her. For one thing, as soon as she became betrothed, she began to wear a veil. Like an engagement ring, it signified to all other men that she was "taken," for now she was regarded as a wife. This squelched all other prospective marriage offers. As far as her availability to other men was concerned, she might as well be dead. She was spoken of as being "sanctified," or set apart, for the exclusive use of her husband.

She began to collect what we would refer to as a trousseau. Her bridal garments were purchased or painstakingly sewn, the sense of urgency heightened by the fact that neither she nor her bridegroom knew the deadline against which they both worked.

For the bride, this waiting period provided a time for her to prepare herself for her new role. She had to begin to consciously transfer her allegiance from her father to her husband, from what was familiar to someone who was mysterious and comparatively unknown. She had to accustom herself to the idea of depending physically on someone to provide for her needs, among them shelter and clothing. She was also learning, in response, to share herself with him. She knew she would never be able to match him, either in the bride-price he'd paid for her nor in his physical strength, so the idea of any repayment could never enter her mind. All she could do would be to set her mind to pleasing him, to making him happy that he had chosen her to share his life.

For his part, he would work joyously on that symbol of his dreams, the bridal chamber, fulfilling that ancestral urge to build that his forebears had always exhibited. Like Noah whose first act out of the ark was to construct an altar; like David aching for a wood-and-stone temple for his God; like countless generations who set up boundary markers and spent time in booths for remembrance; the young Jewish bridegroom was programmed by his heritage with one cathartic response to his emotions. Build something. And so he did.

Each stitch on the wedding garment, every nail in the bridal chamber—they only marked time into measurable segments of accomplishment that made the seemingly interminable waiting bearable for the young man and woman who longed to be one.

### Our Betrothal to Christ

Like the young bride of Bible times, Christ's own bride, His church, has been relatively passive in the betrothal process. We, individually and collectively, have been chosen by Him without our prior knowledge, but not without our permission.

Like the young bride, we have been offered a chance to accept His offer of union. We have been made acutely aware of the high cost to Him and stand in awe of the fact that He has already unflinchingly paid it, in full. But He is ever aware of the cost to us of ratifying that commitment, of drinking from that cup.

James and John once urged Him to let them have a special place in His kingdom. "You don't know what you're asking," He responded. "Can you drink from the cup I am going to drink?" This conversation between three Jewish men wasn't a frivolous one. To drink from the same cup meant a contract. It meant "no matter what." It meant "I'll fulfill my word, even at the cost of my life." The brimming bride cup that He offers us means no less. With it, He demonstrates the finality of His sacrifice, His salute to His bride, and His pledge of fidelity.

Our acceptance of Christ as our betrothed spouse is spoken of in the Bible as an accomplished fact. Paul saw himself as an on-going matchmaker between Christ and the church, a chaperon of our virtue during this waiting period. "I am jealous for you with godly jealousy," he wrote in 2 Corinthians 11:2. "I [promised] you to one husband that I may present you as a chaste virgin to Christ."

Thus Christ has, like the Old Testament bridegroom, become our husband, even before the actual nuptials. This union is as indissoluble as the eventual marriage, for our Spouse has given up all rights to ever divorce us, and has taken away even the ability of death to part us: He overcame death, and we will too. If we are married to the Lord, we will never be widowed.

Like the young bride of Bible times, we live on promises and whatever signs we see that He is fulfilling them. After our Husband paid the bride-price for us, He made a promise that continues to hearten us when nothing else can: He said He was going to begin to prepare a mansion for us. We can't hear the sound of the hammering, but we comfort each other with the thought of the furnishings and provisions. And we know that each passing day He delays His coming means another day He is preparing for us, waiting for His Father to say that everything is finally ready.

Each day of delay, too, gives us more precious time to prepare for Him. Obedience becomes a pleasurable act when we realize the truth of Barclay's statement that "to disobey God is like breaking the marriage vow. It means that all sin is sin against love . . . when we sin, we break God's heart." We look for new ways to make ourselves pleasing and beautiful to Him, knowing that he doesn't look on the outward appearance, but on our hearts. We seek out new skills that will make us more "at home" in heaven: love, joy, peace, giving.

It's no wonder that those outside the church don't understand us. They see the veil, the visible difference between us and them, and know that it means something, but they cannot always identify its significance. They understand that we are spoken for, that we seem unmoved by—indeed, almost dead to—certain other allurements, but they cannot see the absent Bridegroom except as the joy our faces reflect. With a shrug, they give us unwittingly one of the greatest compliments the world can give

when they say, "That's just the way they are." And the way we are
is holy, set apart, sanctified, possessed. They can see that.

Of course, this process of becoming His possession takes
time. We, like the young bride, must continually evaluate our
allegiances, transferring our loyalties from our old ways and
wants, to Him. And like the young bride, we know that we can
never think of being able to repay Him for He does not want what
we can give, but what we can be.

It pleases us, reaffirms our feelings about love, when we
realize that Christ is moved in a similar way to action in order to
show His love for us. The mental picture of Him and His Father
working (John 5:17) is thrilling to our minds. The prospect of
living as His bride in a mansion he has lovingly constructed is
beyond our comprehension.

We do not chafe behind the veil we must wear. We know
that it is a divine pledge of commitment. But it is also a temporary thing that will one day be removed by His loving hand when
we will "know as we are known." We stand shoulder to shoulder
with Thomas, blessed because we believe without seeing; arm in
arm with Peter's friends who haven't seen Him, yet nonetheless
love Him.

Our faith is not based on the sound of the hammer on the
roof of the bride chamber, nor secured by the wealth of the bride-
price, nor slaked by the cup we long ago drank from. These are all
elements of that covenant, but they pale in the light of the Person
who promised.

He who promised is, above all, faithful. He will come back
for us.

# Chapter 6

## *The* Mohar

The story is told of a primitive culture where brides were purchased from their parents using cattle as an exchange medium. An average woman might merit the bride-price of two cattle, an exceptional woman might bring three; while a less desirable woman's family would receive one cow.

Into this society, the story goes, a rich and attractive suitor came, looking for a wife. All the families paraded their eligible daughters before him. Everyone was surprised when he announced his intention to negotiate with the family of a young woman who was unattractive and clumsy.

*Perhaps it's a bargain he's after,* the townspeople speculated, wondering if perhaps he would offer chickens instead of cows. To everyone's amazement, he offered the girl's family six cows for their daughter and quickly whisked her away for a long honeymoon.

When they returned, months later, no one recognized the new bride. Gone were the slumping shoulders and dull eyes. It was as if she were a new person, radiating beauty and confidence.

No, her husband had not bought her beauty treatments or a facelift. He had begun their relationship by showing her in a tangible way that he thought she was important and valuable. She had begun to act the part, to see herself as he saw her, and the rest of her life she was viewed with awe by all her friends—a six-cow woman.

The Jews of Bible times would have understood this story very well, for the practice of paying a bride-price to a girl's parents was a deeply imbedded custom. They called this price a *mohar,* a word which appears three times in the Old Testament (Genesis 34:12, Exodus 22:17, and 1 Samuel 18:25).

48                                                    THE *MOHAR*

The word *mohar* means simply "price," but its special usage in marriage customs gave it a unique significance which tied its usage almost exclusively to marriage. Just the opposite has happened with our word wedding. Through the years, it has lost its original meaning, for the "wed" was originally the money or property that a man offered as security on his pledge to marry a woman, and a "wedding" was the completion of that vow.

### *Determining the* Mohar

The price paid for a bride in Bible times was determined largely by the social standing of the girl's family. Her appearance and characteristics, of course, would have influenced this price, but when we remember that many girls were betrothed at a very young age, these were not usually given great weight unless she had some ongoing physical or emotional problems.

The only mention of a definite money price for a bride is found in Deuteronomy 22:29, that of fifty shekels of silver (if silver is $5.31 per ounce, about $531.00). However, this price is a punitive amount levied on a man who had had sexual relations with an unbetrothed woman and who was thus required to marry her. This was, though, twice the price for a female slave, so even at that this bride's value was high. Later we read in Hosea 3:2 that Hosea paid for his wife the fee of fifteen shekels of silver (about $159.00 today) and about ten bushels of barley—a price that reflected her "shopworn" condition.

The lack of scriptural evidence of a firm bride-price is doubtless a reflection of the fact that this was an area where bargaining was important. We are reminded of the highly developed nature of this art and its attendant etiquette in Genesis 23 when Abraham negotiated for the burial plot for Sarah.

To set a value on a human being was surely a delicate thing, a subjective matter where beauty as always was in the eye of the beholder—and the eyes of his prospective in-laws. A bridegroom would be aware of his own resources and their limitations, while the bride's parents could, on the other hand, argue convincingly (and scripturally!) that a good wife's value was "far above rubies." Just how close the two realities could come to each other determined her actual price.

Often the bride's whole family got in on the act of negotiations, as in the case of Rebekah's betrothal in Genesis 24. A Canaanite poem found at Ras Shamra in Syria paints the vivid picture of the weighing of the bride-price, where the father set the beams of the balance, the mother arranged the trays, the brothers arranged the ingots, while the sisters attended to the stones of the balances.

Sometimes the bride-price was set unreasonably high with the purpose of scaring away an undesirable suitor. Saul, for example, thought he could get rid of young David by setting the *mohar* for his daughter Michal as the foreskins of one hundred Philistines. So great was David's enthusiasm and battle prowess, however, that he brought back double that number, and in the process not only fulfilled the king's requirement but unwittingly made himself more a threat to the king than ever before.

David, who had characterized himself as "only a poor man, and little known," was not the only Bible suitor who didn't have money for a *mohar* for the wife he wanted. Moses' help with the flocks of Jethro apparently earned Zipporah, and Jacob worked a total of fourteen years for his beloved Rachael.

Other men earned their wives as David did through heroic battle deeds. Caleb offered his daughter to whoever captured the city of Kiriah Sepher, and his nephew Othniel rose to the occasion. Another man, Shechem, agreed to an equally hazardous venture as a condition of his marriage. He and all the males of his city were circumcised as a prerequisite to his betrothal to Dinah.

If all else failed, a poor man with no battle skills or marketable craft might convince his community to take up a collection to help him and his family with a *mohar*. The thinking was, apparently, that a quality wife would enhance the entire community and was thus worth the cash outlay.

## *The Purpose of the* Mohar

Not only could a daughter not carry on the family name for the father, she received no military training in order to defend the family in wartime. And daughters did little to contribute to any family business that involved heavy labor. A man with many sons had a long-term work force whose wages were dinner; a man with many daughters had to feed them and hire laborers, too. When a woman married, she became part of someone else's family, perhaps moving far away and thus becoming unable to help her parents in their old age as a son was expected to do.

In Bible times, therefore, the birth of a daughter meant an extended financial drain on a family. The only way a family could recoup these losses was by raising daughters who would bring a good *mohar*. Keeping young women healthy, chaste and serviceably trained to be wives and mothers was undoubtedly a challenging proposition and parents felt they earned every single shekel. By offering a more-than-modest *mohar*, too, a suitor showed that he was capable of supporting his bride. Understandably, no parents would knowingly allow a daughter to enter a marriage where she would face starvation or bondage.

A second purpose for the *mohar* was that it served as a kind of "earnest money" that guaranteed the bridegroom's sincerity and allayed the fears of the parents who took their daughter out of the marriage marketplace for him. It showed that he knew not to expect to get "something for nothing."

By leaving the *mohar* with the parents, he also laid a foundation for trust in their relationship. Nothing but their mutual word of honor would prevent the parents from absconding with the *mohar*—like the proverbial Arabs, folding up their literal tents and stealing away into an anonymous sunset, there to re-market their lucrative daughter.

### *The Results of the* Mohar

There were no firm rules about how the parents were bound to use the *mohar* money once they received it from the bridegroom. Some of it was undoubtedly used to prepare for the upcoming wedding. Surprisingly, though, most or all of the money was often given directly to the bride in the form of her dowry, which will be discussed in the next chapter.

The *mohar*, then, was often considered by a bride to be her own personal property. This is aptly illustrated in Genesis 31, where Rachael and Leah complained against Laban. They felt betrayed by their trickster father who had both played on the emotions of Jacob by substituting the weak-eyed Leah for Rachael but had also required him to work an additional seven years for Rachael. That obligation paid, their father was still dipping his hand into their family finances by changing Jacob's wages and breaking agreements about flock allocations. Their most serious grievance against their father, though, was that he had not only "sold" them, but had used up their *mohar* (verse 15). In the King James Version, the daughters refer to this money as "their" money, something over which they felt that he had no rights.

The fact that two women would say such a thing should dispel many of the current theories that women in the Old Testament had no legal or financial value. Indeed, one of the most significant results of the *mohar* system was this: It showed that a woman had an inherent, even measurable and marketable worth in her society. She was not chattel to be auctioned off to the highest bidder but rather an important ingredient whose suitability in a marriage was to be carefully weighed, and dearly paid for.

The woman who witnessed the exchange of the *mohar* for her promise to marry someone could only come to one conclusion: she must be special for him to pay such a price. Of course, the higher the price, the more her feelings of self-worth must have increased; and the more determined she must have felt to live up to his trust in her by being the wife he expected, and that his *mohar* had purchased.

### The Mohar of Christ

There has been a bride-price paid for Christ's bride, the church. We, the set-apart betrothed, have been bought with a price, a *mohar* that is unlike any ever negotiated for in the history of the world. Like any other *mohar,* its value was determined by the worth of the bride—but for the only time in history, the bride's soiled condition, her utter unredeemability, pushed the bride-price extortionately high.

Our Lover, Jesus, worked long and hard for us—thirty-three years of earthtime. He fought heroically in the most crucial battle ever waged. He suffered pain that makes the debilitating circumcision of Shechem seem insignificant.

The *mohar* He offered was the deep, sparkling red of His own blood. Both Acts 20:28 and 1 Peter 1:18–19 speak of this blood almost as a commodity, a medium of exchange in a negotiation for the church.

Other scriptures, though, speak of this contractual deal as something more than a situation where both parties were sitting calmly across from each other over a friendly flagon of wine. When we speak of redeeming something, we think of a payment for something that is temporarily out of our control: a garment in lay-away, subject to restocking if we do not make the deadline; or a ring pawned to cover bills before payday.

Even more descriptive is the word "ransom." It brings to mind thoughts of someone who has been taken away by force and is in imminent personal danger. The ransom must be paid without question and without demands. Peter used this word to describe what Christ did for us in 1 Timothy 2:6, and Jesus Himself used the same term to describe His very purpose on this earth. He knew He had come, quite simply, in exchange for people in trouble, people who could not help themselves; people more unlovely than the six-cow woman before her marriage; people who could offer Him nothing in return, not even companionship as He paid the ransom in a dark rendezvous for their very souls.

If it was a ransom, then, to whom was it paid? Many have speculated that this price was paid to Satan since he was our spiritual father before our redemption. But God owes that old serpent nothing, nor does Jesus owe him anything for us. Satan's rule over us is only temporary. In this situation, the church is the child of her heavenly Father, her Creator, and the bride-price, like the temple sacrifices, was made payable only to Him.

When we speak of the cost of this *mohar* we speak in terms of blood, the currency that Leviticus tells us is the common denominator of the elusive thing we call life. When we say, "Jesus paid it all," we are also saying that Jesus paid His all—for He, like us, had only one life to give. He bankrupted Himself for us.

The book of Hebrews repeatedly uses the word "offered" in conjunction with the idea of Christ's sacrifice, and our twentieth-century ears hear in that word the echo of a business transaction, a bid for something desired. Like the bridegrooms of old, Christ left His offering "on the table," trusting that the bride would keep her end of the bargain and be there for Him when He returned for her.

We cannot, we must not, forget that this Jewish Son had some questions about this transaction and His own ability to fulfill it. Just before He submitted the *mohar* of His life, He had an earnest discussion with His Father. He asked if there were any other way this contract could be finalized than by drinking from the coming cup. The Son was asking the Father, "Is this *mohar* too high? Is there any other way she can be earned?" But in the end, He, the obedient Son, deferred to His Father's judgment, His Father's will.

The cost was high. A lesser bridegroom would have been frightened away forever by its exorbitance, but like Jacob He was motivated by a love that made the time seem short. Like David, His desire for His bride made the bride-price worthwhile.

When the payment came due, He was resolved and ready. Stripped naked, He stretched out gasping on a splintered cross, the drops of His *mohar* dripping rhythmically onto the ground until the full price was extracted.

We, His bride, are awed by the sense of self-worth that this price paid gives us. We are reaffirmed by our "market value" and our inaccessibility to other suitors.

Others in the world, though not yet part of this transaction, see the difference in a bride who knows her priceless worth to her Lover. Like the family of Rebekah, they are recipients of our reflected joy, the liberally dispensed gifts and happiness.

Has it been worth it, the price of this *mohar,* to the Bridegroom?

The question might better be asked:

Has the bride yet made Him glad He went through with it?

# Chapter 7

## Two Gifts to the Bride

The *mohar* that changed hands surely would have made the young bride of Bible times feel a great sense of value and dignity. But as any modern-day professional athlete would agree, there is quite a lot of difference between a price that is exchanged on your behalf, and a gift which is given to you directly. Knowing that you have a high market value is one thing; holding the proceeds from such a transaction in your hands is another thing altogether.

### *The* Mattan

Sometime near the end of the betrothal period the young Jewish bride would be given a gift by her parents. This was called a *mattan,* or dowry. As the previous chapter pointed out, this *mattan* was often funded by the *mohar* that her future husband had given her parents as the bride-price. As that chapter also pointed out in the case of Rachael and Leah, this *mattan* was something that was ideally the exclusive property of the bride herself. While ostensibly a show of favor from parent to child, the *mattan* had a very utilitarian function. It would remain in her possession, "in trust," against the day when she might be widowed or even worse, deserted or divorced by her husband.

In those days when there were no insurance policies or Social Security, the *mattan* was a necessary part of the financial structure of a community. If a bride's parents were for some reason unable to provide her with a suitable dowry, often the community would provide one—with a kind of "pay me now or pay me later" attitude. By so doing, they could prevent her social humiliation now as well as her being a potential drain on the town's economy later.

It has often been maintained by those who have studied the role of women in Bible times that wives differed from material property only in the fact that they, unlike possessions, could not be sold. But the *mattan* [dowry] must have had the function of elevating her social status, for it made her, like her husband, a property owner.

Early in the history of God's people, certain women were indeed able to own and to inherit property. We see this in the book of Job, where that patriarch gave his daughters an inheritance just like their brothers. The daughters of Zelophehad, too, are singled out in scripture as examples of women who inherited directly from their father.

But by the time of Ruth, conditions and attitudes had apparently changed, for we see Naomi and her two daughters-in-law destitute, unable to claim the estate of Naomi's dead husband until one of his kinsmen redeemed and claimed it (and Ruth).

Barclay tells us that at one time in Jewish history women were actually refusing to marry because the thinking of that time allowed the man to appropriate the woman's *mattan* as his own, to spend as he wished. Then the easy divorce laws allowed him to desert her, penniless and without any legal recourse. Simon ben Shetah enacted a new ecclesiastical law wherein the dowry, then called the *Kethubah,* could indeed be spent or invested by the husband. But were he ever to divorce his wife, he must repay the *Kethubah* to her—even if he had to "sell his own hair" to do so. This had two immediate effects: more women were willing to marry, and more men were unwilling to divorce. But it still did not return the full rights of the dowry to the wife as was originally intended.

## *Types of Gifts in the* Mattan

The fact that the *mattan* was not always a monetary gift which parents gave to daughters is abundantly illustrated in the Old Testament. The earliest example we have was Rebekah's mother and uncle sending her off to her new husband with her nurse,

56 TWO GIFTS TO THE BRIDE

Deborah. Deborah was apparently a wonderful *mattan,* a valued and trusted servant of the family, for when she died, the tree beneath which she was buried was poignantly named "the oak of weeping."

Caleb presented his daughter with a *mattan* of a tract of land in the Negev. Later he added immeasurably to the value of that arid land by also giving her rights to upper and lower springs of water. In another example in 1 Kings 9 we read how Pharaoh attacked, captured, set on fire and killed the Canaanite inhabitants of the city of Gezer. He then presented this *mattan* to his daughter, the wife of Solomon, as a wedding gift. (Apparently Solomon was nonplussed at this "burnt offering," because he went on to rebuild Gezer.)

Apparently a very common *mattan* was the gift of a handmaid. Such a servant was obviously invaluable in taking care of all the household tasks that a woman of the Old Testament had to do. The Scriptures show that these handmaids filled a need for their mistresses who were barren: that of providing children for the mistresses' husbands. Clay tablets found in the sixteenth century B.C. city of Nuzi show that the laws of this northern Mesopotamian culture allowed such a practice, and venerable women of the Bible availed themselves of it.

When Sarah, for example, urged Abraham to sleep with her maid Hagar, she did so with the thought that any child born of such a union would legally be Sarah's. When Rachael's servant Bilhah bore a son to Jacob, Rachael triumphantly announced, "God has given me a son." Whatever the feelings we experience when we consider such a claim, we must admit that these matriarchs regarded the handmaids which were their *mattan* as personal property, and claimed any child born to such servants as their own. In Genesis 30:3 the statement, "Bilhah shall bear upon my knees . . ." was a way of saying the child shall be legally mine.

### *Our* Mattan *Today*

Even today the practice of a dowry is an important part of many cultures of the world. As in the ancient world, the amount and type of the dowry says much about the bride and her parents. A recent Associated Press newspaper story detailed how hundreds of young women in India each year are burned to death by their husbands or their mothers-in-law because these relatives regard the dowry that the young women brought to the marriage to be inadequate. Those in this situation who are not burned alive or beaten to death are often subjected to threats, abuse and torture in the homes of their in-laws where most Indian brides live. To this culture, the dowry is a vitally important issue.

Probably the closest parallel to the Old Testament idea of a *mattan* that would provide security to a wife is seen in the fact that most parents would urge—and pay for—a young woman's education before marriage so that in the event of that marriage's termination, she may support herself and any children. While we in the Western world regard the idea of a dowry as something outdated, our contemporary practices still show vestiges of this old, old custom. Many parents contribute to their daughters' trousseaus or hope chests. Others "help out" by buying appliances, insurance policies, or even a few months' rent on the newlyweds' apartment.

As Christians, though, we delight to think on the *mattan* that our Heavenly Father has provided for us. We are betrothed to His Son, and He is a loving and giving Parent.

How unlike the god of a man I met in Bombay, India! There in the lobby of the Taj Mahal Hotel I spoke with a Hong Kong businessman who was a member of a religion that claimed over 100,000 followers. He related how he, and his ancestors, had kept a continual fire burning for over 700 years in the temple of his deity. He had worshiped and served this god all his life. "But I have no peace," he admitted. The reason was that his god was insensate to everything except receiving. For hundreds of years, this man's people had, out of fear and obligation, served a god who could not bestow blessings, who could not communicate and who could not even provide peace of mind. His god knew only how to take.

James tells us that our God is a Father who bestows many gifts on us—indeed, that every good and perfect gift we have is from Him (1:17). Leah in the Old Testament recognized this. Though she had brought both money and her handmaid Zilpah to her marriage to Jacob as a *mattan* from her father Laban, she also acknowledged another *mattan* from her heavenly Father—what the KJV calls the "dowry" of a son.

How rich our dowry and how beyond recounting, and yet we strain to attempt the telling. Sometimes even the obvious escapes us—the fact that God is the author of our very lives, the breath we respire that allows us to continue even our worship to Him, "in whom we live and move and have our being."

Not only is life a gift but so is individuality—the fact that He created us a race, yet each different. Like the Rembrandt painting that recently sold for over a million dollars, we are the work of Genius, each one of a kind, signed with His likeness.

The enabling of breath, the ennobling of entity: these alone might have sufficed a lesser Parent. But dissatisfied with only these, He decided to share Himself with all mankind through the Holy Spirit, pouring Him out onto us, drenching us with His constant presence.

The Spirit, Himself a gift, serves to remind us of many other dowry-gifts the Father offers to the bride. First among these is grace. Only because of it, and through it, can Christ love such an unlovable bride. Only because He has chosen to see us through the rose-tinted glasses of grace can we ourselves overlook our blemishes and imperfections; no other "beauty treatment" from our Father could so prepare us for our wedding day.

Many of the gifts which accompany us on our way to our wedding are the promises God has made to us. Like the *mattan* of the Jewish bride they are literally held in trust by us against the day when we can redeem those promises. God's "gift" of eternal life (Romans 6:23), for instance, is like an insurance policy against the uncertainties of this life. Also, the unearned salvation that Paul referred to as a "gift" in Ephesians 2:8, gives us comfort and security no matter how lonely or long this betrothal period may seem.

These dowry gifts, we must constantly remind ourselves, are not ours because of any merit we have, or any debt that the Father owes us. He "en-dowers" (endows) us with them with the same motivations as the Bible fathers did: because we need them and because He is our Father.

Christians so endowed are the richest of all people, and yet we live like the children of paupers, benighted as to our great wealth. We are like the man in Texas who lived on his tract of land, near bankruptcy until a great oil strike on his land. Now he lives in comfort—not because he has any more oil than before, but because he knows it, and knows how to use it.

We needn't fear that God will suddenly or capriciously ask for any of these gifts back. Romans 11:29 comforts us with the fact that both God's calling, and His gifts, are irrevocable. No more than the Old Testament father would burst into his daughter's bedroom and demand her *mattan* back, would our heavenly Father take back those gifts which He has lovingly prepared for our use since time began.

## The Bridegroom's Gift to the Bride

Besides the *mattan,* or dowry, that the bride received for her marriage, she also was given a special gift by the bridegroom himself. Like the dowry, it was to be her exclusive possession. Because it could not be used by her husband, and because it was a source of security for her, someone once termed this gift "alimony in advance."

There are only two Old Testament examples of this gift. One occurs in the betrothal of Isaac to Rebekah, where she was given gold and silver jewelry and articles of clothing. The other is found in Genesis 34, in the account of the betrothal of Jacob's daughter Dinah to Shechem. In verse 12 Shechem agrees to bring both a bride-price (*mohar*) as well as a gift. (This verse is interesting because it is the only place in the Bible where both are mentioned together.)

A third possible example of a bridegroom's gift is found in the story of Esther. However, it is not clear from the scriptural account whether any of the gifts the king distributed at the time of the holiday that celebrated his wedding, gifts given "with royal liberality" (Esther 2:18), were for his bride. But the fact that they were given in honor of her is obvious.

The New Testament, however, has a striking and unforgettable story about a bridegroom's gift that is found among the parables of Jesus. It is the story found in Luke 15 about the woman
searching for her lost coin.

Jewish houses of Jesus' day were often dark and cramped,
with a mud-and-straw floor that made a small object seem to
disappear when dropped. We can imagine a woman, stooping in
the feeble light afforded by the single, round window in her home,
searching frantically for a coin. She would immediately light a
lamp, and then look for her broom so that she could carefully
sweep even the darkest corners.

Of course, part of her concern would be financial. Such a
coin was probably a silver drachma, representative of a whole day's
wages for a working man of the time. It might represent dawn-to-
dusk grueling labor in the fields or at a quarry or in a vineyard.

But it wasn't just any silver drachma that she was looking
for. It was part of a headdress of ten such coins, attached to a
silver chain, that she wore along with her veil to show she was
married, much as we wear a wedding ring. She cherished it because it enhanced her beauty, and proved her social standing, but
most of all because it had been a gift from her husband.

Of all her physical possessions, this and her dowry were
inalienably hers. The headdress could not be taken from her,
even to pay a family debt. Without the lost silver coin, its beauty
was marred, its design incomplete. With this knowledge, we can
understand why Jesus related the woman's plight between the
story of the loss of a sheep who was integrally part of a flock, and
the loss of a son without whom a family was lacking.

Of course the shepherd, who knew each little lamb, was
willing to go and look for the one hundredth sheep. Of course the
father stood looking with an aching heart for his son. And of
course the woman felt reaffirmed as a woman and as a wife when
she could once again wear her coin headdress, the badge of her
marriage and of her husband's love for her.

### Christ's Gifts to His Bride

In Norway, a bridegroom has the custom of presenting his new
wife with a gift, usually of jewelry, the morning after their nuptial

night. The message is the tender thought that not only was she worth marrying, she is worth keeping.

He could say that because he knows the bride now. We, as the bride of Christ, anxiously await the day when we can know Him, even as He already knows us. The fact that we have no secrets from our Bridegroom might fill us with fears were it not for the fact that He has already given us His gifts of approval.

Ephesians 4:8, quoting from Psalm 68:18, tells us that He has indeed given us gifts. Verse eleven identifies some of those gifts as His enabling of individuals to serve the corporate body, the Bride. Their purpose? To prepare us all for works of service, to build up the body, to promote unity of the faith and, most of all, to help us know our Bridegroom better and better as we mature.

First Corinthians 12–14 is more specific about the mechanisms by which the church is built up, and they, too, are called gifts. They have been provided by a loving Bridegroom who wants His bride to feel secure and able to handle the day-to-day affairs of her relationship with Him.

Paul said in 1 Corinthians 1:5 that we have been enriched in every way. We do not lack any spiritual gift. The Greek word for "enriched" is *ploutos,* and we indeed are plutocrats in the gifts that Christ has presented us with: leaders and abilities that make our lives richer. Just as the headdress of silver coins marked the wife in Luke 15, so our possession of and wise use of Christ's gifts to us mark us as His.

We rest secure against the future, for these gifts are just a fraction of what He plans to give us. All our needs will be met, Philippians 4 promises, according to God's glorious riches in His Son, Christ Jesus.

### The Earnest

How can we be sure of this?

Well, He made a down payment on all His promises. The Scriptures call this an earnest, like the earnest money we put down when we buy a house. This deposit guarantees that the transaction will take place.

The Scriptures use the Greek word *arrabon* for this concept. In the Septuagint this word is employed in the Genesis account of how Judah left his seal, staff and cord as a pledge, or earnest, to guarantee payment to the young woman he thought was a prostitute. In modern Greek, the derivative word *arrabona* actually means "engagement ring."

But the New Testament uses the word *arrabon* for a much superior earnest, for a far loftier purpose. That *arrabon* is not a what, but a Who—the Holy Spirit. Like the dowry, this earnest is a gift from the Father. The presence of the Spirit in our hearts accompanies His seal of ownership on us (2 Corinthians 1:22), serves as a deposit (2 Corinthians 5:5) and guarantees that God will not renege on His promises, change His mind or give our inheritance to anyone else (Ephesians 1:14).

The presence of this Spirit, sweetly indwelling the Bride and quietly counseling her, is as obvious to the spiritually discerning as the meaning of the silver headdress was to those who lived by the customs of the Jews.

As long as the Spirit is here, the promise stands. We have the assurance that we will indeed enter that nuptial tent where all barriers will fall, where we will see as we have been seen, and know as we have been known, and rejoice, and rejoice.

# Chapter 8

## *The Wedding Party*

If there were an Emily Post of Bible times, we regret her disappearance from the pages of history, for we are bereft of any assurance of certainty as we trace the agenda of a Jewish wedding. Though Scripture has abundant references to wedding celebrations, it is totally silent about the order of the events of such—and almost as mute about much of the protocol.

This is doubly complicated by the fact that wedding customs varied from age to age, and from locality to locality. An example of this is seen in the betrothal of Joseph and Mary. In Galilee, where they resided at that time, a woman was forbidden to have any direct contact with her betrothed until her wedding day. In other times, indeed even in neighboring communities of the same time, women were not nearly so restricted.

The same variation of customs was also true in the length of the betrothal period. For instance, the betrothal period during the time of Rebekah was just the time it took her to travel from her homeland on camelback to the home of her husband, Isaac. However, by Talmudic times (2nd cent. A.D.), the betrothal's length had become standardized: one year for a virgin, three months for a widow.

The reasoning for this was clear: a virgin, in the secure household of her father, could afford the year of waiting and perhaps even needed that time for preparations. A widow, on the other hand, might not be financially able to wait that long. Once such a decision had been made, the sooner the marriage the better for her.

Even the day of the week on which a marriage could take place eventually became a standardized matter. A virgin would always marry on a Wednesday. Again we see the Jewish pragmatism. Since the Jewish courts of law convened on Thursdays, if a man discovered that his bride was indeed no virgin, he could divorce her immediately—the very next day. A widow, in contrast, would marry on a Thursday, because no such expectations of virginity (or litigation for lack of such) were anticipated.

### The End of the Betrothal

So, therefore, the young Jewish bride had some signposts by which to gauge the length of her betrothal. The interim between the betrothal and the "taking" of her as wife (Deuteronomy 20:7), while uncertain, was assuredly both finite and somewhat resolvable. While she could not know exactly when, she did know that her wedding would take place sometime around the completion of about a year's betrothal; on some Wednesday. And if the groom had his way, it would be at a time when she least expected it.

Matthew 22 gives us some insights into the mechanics of how such a feat was engineered. As we mentioned in the chapter dealing with the betrothal, the father of the groom was the one who made the final decision on when the wedding would take place. Apparently some fathers did not even take their sons into their confidence until the last minute. But meanwhile, the father would be keeping a close eye on two things: his son's progress on the bridal chamber, and his own finances. The latter was important, because a family's social standing in a community and their reputation depended on the lavishness of the coming celebrations. Some rabbis even allowed that a family's precious Torah scroll could be sold to pay for a daughter's wedding.

When both the bridal chamber and the father's situation seemed ready, the father would begin preparations for the wedding festivities by sending out a preliminary invitation to the prospective wedding guests. As Matthew 22 illustrates, there was no set time mentioned in this first communication: it was more like an "alert" than an actual invitation. The urgent summons to come would be later, when the dinner was actually prepared, the fattened animals butchered. Even today, orthodox Jews consider it necessary to have two invitations to a formal gathering, because to them one summons alone is not valid. In Esther 5:8 the first invitation to the banquet was sent out and in 6:14 the second invitation was extended. The second was to invite those previously called.

The idea of sending out messengers at the last minute is a method still very much alive in many parts of the world. I once arrived in Bangalore, India, late on a Wednesday evening in preparation for speaking to a group there on Friday, Saturday and Sunday. I was asked to speak a day early, on Thursday, but I replied that this would be impossible, because most of the members had no telephones by which they could know of the change in plans. But the hardy pastor there hopped onto his bicycle, pedaling furiously to all the surrounding areas, telling members as well as strangers of the Thursday meeting. It was announced all day long and right up to the time of the meeting, which was, in the end, very well attended.

Of course, the communications system used in Bible times was even less efficient. But still the rumors of an impending marriage would leak out. A bride's relatives and friends might report to her the finishing touches on the bridal chamber; a butcher friend might drop hints that the bridegroom's father was on the lookout for a fine fatted calf; some special material might be on order at the local tailor's; a wine shipment would arrive auspiciously in the town; and the year would draw maddeningly to a close for the young bride.

Besides her personal preparations, the bride was also spending these last days carefully selecting those special young women who would be her marriage companions, or maidens (Psalm 45:9,14; Song of Solomon 1:5; 2:7; 3:5; 8:4). Sisters and close friends were undoubtedly the candidates; and, once chosen, the young women would come with increasing frequency to the bride's home during the evenings.

There they would giggle and speculate and gossip and sing the special songs called the *epithaleneum* to while the time away. (Some scholars have speculated that the Song of Solomon was in fact a collection of such *epithaleneum.*) Of course, on a Tuesday evening (remember that the Jewish day Wednesday began at sundown on Tuesday), all the bride's friends would unfailingly be at her home on the chance that this might be *the* day.

Near the end of the betrothal year, many an anxious bride would even dress in her wedding garment these evenings, just to be sure. It probably was richly embroidered (Psalm 45:14), bright (Revelation 19:8), with a luxurious belt or girdle (Isaiah 49:18). All around her would be the fragrant aroma of myrrh, aloes and cassia (Psalm 45:8). She would be wearing all the jewels she could afford or borrow. Her friends would braid her long hair for her, interweaving it with jewels if possible.

We can so easily visualize such a young girl, literally sitting at the edge of her seat or pacing to keep her beautiful gown free from spots or wrinkles. The gown itself might be a gift from her groom (Ezekiel 16:10), and, if so, she would be especially careful to keep it neat. And of course she would keep nearby her veil, the symbol of her coming marriage.

She and her companions would stay up far into the night, and her chambers would be filled with laughter and tears as the girls encouraged each other while the bridegroom delayed. They would challenge each other to stay awake, but as the parable of the ten virgins shows, many times they all nodded off to sleep by midnight.

### The Abduction

Of course, nothing could please the bridegroom more than to catch his bride unawares—that was part of the fun. He, too, had been selecting some close friends—known, in fact, as "the friends of the bridegroom" (John 3:29; Judges 14:11,20; Song of Solomon 5:1; 8:13; Matthew 3:29; 9:14). They would serve as his chosen escorts on that great night he was anticipating.

In Judea, one friend in particular had special responsibilities. He was the *shoshben,* or what we would call the "best man." Barclay tells us that he not only served as a liaison between the bride and groom during the betrothal, but also was often entrusted with the delivery of the invitations. He would personally escort the bridegroom to his bride's house and bring them together. Later, at the wedding, he would guard the bridal chamber so no false lover could enter, and he would open the door to only the sound of his friend, the groom's, voice. Thus he was in a very special way the guardian of the virtue of the bride.

When that special night finally came, and the father told his son he could finally go and get his bride, how great the groom's excitement must have been! He and his friends too must be richly attired for this festive occasion. Often, if the groom's family was wealthy, they would provide new, special robes for guests. Just before he would depart, the groom's mother would present him with a special headdress—called in various Bible translations a garland or turban or crown (Song of Solomon 3:11; Psalm 110:3; Isaiah 61:10, 62:5; Revelation 11:15). This lovely custom of wearing a wedding crown, however, disappeared after the destruction of Jerusalem—perhaps in deference to that catastrophe.

Thus royally attired, the excited young groom would set out from his home with a flourish that David once compared to a spectacular sunrise (Psalm 19:5). The stillness of the Judean night would be broken by the frantic assembling of his entourage, the glad sounds of musicians and singers hired for the occasion, and tear-choked farewells from his proud parents.

All throughout his village, people would be awakened from their sleep by the wedding party's joyous sounds. "Everyone from six to sixty," a Jewish saying went, "will follow the marriage drum." Indeed, the wedding party's noise was soon compounded by families awakening and peering out windows at the commotion. The always-present village dogs barked, cattle lowed, babies cried. Such an occasion was not an everyday affair and so many who did not actually join the bridal procession made a mental note of the bridegroom's identity so they could drop by later at the feast. Even the ever-essential study of the law, the rabbis said, could be put aside temporarily for the sake of attending a wedding feast.

Meanwhile the noisy procession was shushed and hushed as it made its approach to the bride's house. While the element of surprise was essential, tradition obliged the wedding party to assign one of the men the task of giving a loud, triumphant shout of warning as they neared the girl's home.

And that was all the warning she got—just enough time for her to light a lamp, put on her veil and reach for her honeymoon clothes. What a scramble that must have been, as the bridesmaids too all awakened, each quickly preparing to leave and looking for her own lamp that would be such a necessity on those rough village streets.

With the rowdy party of men outside practically storming the door, there remained but one last detail that must be attended to. The bride's parents would give their daughter a quick, final embrace and pronounce over her a standardized blessing which had as its source the farewell benediction given to Rebekah (Genesis 24:60) and that of Ruth (Ruth 4:11–12): an expression of love and a desire that the marriage would be successful and fruitful. Indeed, the Jewish parents were in a very real way surrendering their daughter to her bridegroom, for the moment that she stepped out of their doorway to go with him, she ceased to be part of their family and became a part of her new husband's tribe and clan.

But this short ritual took only a few moments. Outside, the party grew louder and more boisterous. Keeping her veil close around her, the young bride searched the face of the one for whom she had waited so long. Could this be a dream?

Whether he would say the words of Solomon to his Shulammite bride, or not, did not matter. His eyes would tell her.

"Arise, come, my darling; my beautiful one, come with me."

Then she followed him outside to this midnight beginning of the rest of her life.

### Our Betrothal's End

It seems almost cruel to leave our little Jewish bride here, but we must not neglect the rich implications of her situation that apply to us; for we are, after all, that bride. In our search for Beulah land (for Beulah, Isaiah 62:4–5 tells us, means married), we need to make the necessary preparations for our trip.

As Christians, we began the day of our betrothal—our conversion to Christ—to transfer our citizenship from this household where we now live to the home of our bridegroom

(Philippians 3:20). Though we still reside here, our minds, our hearts, are ever turning toward that future permanent home.

All we have to base this hope on is the promise that the Bridegroom made before He left so many years ago. While He was here on earth, He described Himself with many concrete symbols: Shepherd, Vine, Cornerstone, High Priest, Head, and Last Adam. All of these speak of His caring relationship to us. But only in one symbol, that of bridegroom, is there a return implied. All those promises of the old covenant, and all the glories of the new, will ultimately have no value for us if He cannot, after all, return to vindicate them, and us.

Our ears did not hear those promises. Our eyes did not see Him pay the bride-price, nor prove His power through His resurrection. But like second-generation Thomases we are blessed as we believe in, and love, Him whom we have not seen.

Like the Jewish bride, the bride of Christ is anxiously awaiting the promised return of her Betrothed. We too have prepared our trousseau. We are wearing our wedding gowns, day and night, right now.

In the East, you can easily tell the religion of many people by the clothes they wear. Just as the Sadducees and Pharisees were known by their phylacteries and fringes, today's Sikhs and Buddhist priests are also identified by turbans and saffron robes.

Christ's bride has been clothed with garments that mark us, too. One of these is the clothing of power that was promised in Luke 24:49—that great enabling which the Holy Spirit grants us. Perhaps we could more accurately term it an undergarment or foundation, for though it is not usually visible to outsiders, it is an essential part of our spiritual wardrobe.

The outer apparel of the bride of Christ is clearly pictured in Revelation 19:8, where she is pictured as wearing "fine linen," much as the Jewish bride did. But this linen has a spiritual significance, for it is a symbol, John tells us, of the righteous deeds of the saints. Indeed, sometimes the only thing the rest of the world will remember about us after a brief meeting might be our "clothes"—the deeds of kindness and service we have rendered. Like the Jewish bride, we must be careful not to let this linen become spotted with unChristlike motives or wrinkled through indolence.

Greek legend told of a special cloak, one that allowed its wearer to become invisible. This cloak, when worn, itself became invisible, too. We Christians wear a similar garment, that of salvation, which is never seen except by its effects when worn. The lingering scent it leaves in the air is that of a rose—the sweet aroma of the Rose of Sharon. It has been placed on our shoulders like the garment that a judge would put on a convicted criminal who was acquitted of a crime: a badge of our forgiven status.

We can speak of the garments of righteousness that we wear. We can exult in the fact that they were given to us as a wedding gift like the garments of the bride in Ezekiel 16. But we are jarred by the imagery of a final garment that Paul spoke of in Romans 13:14 and Galatians 3:29; for here the bridal dress we are to wear was not imputed from the bridegroom nor bestowed by Him.

Here He Himself is the garment, and we are told to put Him on and wear Him. Surely no bride in history has been so radiantly robed!

### The Lesson of the Virgins

Jesus' teaching in Matthew 25 about the bride's attendants, or virgins, gives us a vivid understanding of how frustrating and tiring it was to wait for a bridegroom whose arrival time was unknown. But then, again, we don't have to be reminded of how unsettling such uncertainty is, for we are awaiting our bridegroom, too!

Jesus' focus in that parable was not on the bridegroom nor his delay, but on the young virgins themselves. True, He acknowledged that the waiting was very hard (remember, wise and foolish alike fell asleep), but there seems to be no condemnation for the natural weariness that caused their sleep.

They all had good intentions. They all were at the right place at the right time. They all had remembered to bring their lamps.

But half of those young girls were really serious about accompanying the bridegroom. They were not content with bringing along a lamp that would burn steadily for only a short time fed from its reservoir that held only a few teaspoonsful of oil. These young girls wanted to be able to go all the way back to the bridegroom's father's home. They knew they could not make the long walk in the dark. And they knew that a hand-lamp's light was just bright enough for its bearer alone.

With them, as with us, an eternal principle rings true: some situations can't be stopped in mid-frame while we complete our preparations. Some things can't be borrowed or bought. They must be in our possession at the crucial time.

Some of us claim to be waiting for the Bridegroom. We may be singing all the right wedding songs. We can even spend day and night in the bride's house—the church—wearing the "right clothes" of good deeds, and carrying our brightly burning lamps like a badges that will, we think, guarantee our entrance to the wedding.

The Father has sent out the first invitation long ago. The friend of the bridegroom, John the Baptist (John 3:28–30), delivered the first summons, and the Bridegroom Himself continued the ongoing invitation. The Father gave us some good indications of the wedding date, but in the time-honored tradition, promised it would be a surprise.

Even being a good friend of the bride, the parable of the virgins tells us, won't do a bit of good if we can't make it on time to the wedding feast that's been advertised for almost two thousand years. The wedding procession will come and go whether we're in it or frantically beating at the door of a sleepy oil-vender.

"I don't know you," the Bridegroom will say to all the latecomers after His banquet door is locked.

And that will be true. All His friends, the prepared ones, will be inside with Him, rejoicing.

# Chapter 9

## *The Wedding Festivities*

The midnight wedding procession of the young Jewish bride would take the most circuitous route possible in leaving her home and going to the bridegroom's home. This was so that as many people in the village as possible could share in his excitement: a kind of reverse receiving line. The groom himself headed this parade of lights and noisy rejoicing, singing and dancing; leading his heavily veiled bride by the hand.

When they finally arrived in his neighborhood, they stopped at a *huppah,* or bridal canopy, that had been specially erected for this occasion. This consisted of four posts with a canvas or sheet stretched over it, and it was always located out of doors. Various translators of the Bible have translated the term in Joel 2:16 that refers to this canopy as "pavilion," or "bridal chamber" (the word actually means an enclosure or covering), but perhaps "canopy" helps us to understand the structure's function best.

The fact that this canopy was located outside, sometimes even in the village marketplace, is significant for three reasons. First, the structure separated what went on under it from the activities and atmosphere of its mundane surroundings, as if to say: this marriage will be within the day-to-day activities of this village, but will nonetheless always be separate from it. Secondly, the open arrangement of the canopy allowed a maximum number of witnesses at a time to see the bride and groom together. And thirdly, the canopy allowed the wedding party and guests alike to view the star-strewn sky that would remind them of God's promise to father Abraham in Genesis 15—progeny as innumerable as those stars.

Even today the Chinese marry under a canopy they call "the sacred umbrella." And if you visit a Jewish wedding you will see the bride and groom under a *huppah* that will remind them of Rebekah's nuptial tent (Genesis 24:67), as well as their obligation to propagate in the hopes of producing the messiah.

### Over the Threshold

When the bride and groom left the canopy, they completed the process that scripture refers to as "coming together," which refers to the transferral process of the bride from her home to her husband's home. Because of the absence of any certain marriage ceremony (remember, vows and such did not become part of the Jewish marriage ceremony until Roman times), the bride and groom were not actually married until sexual intercourse had taken place.

The site of this occurrence would be the bridal chamber the young groom had worked on during the betrothal period, the "chambers" mentioned in Song of Solomon 1:4. The significance of this entry into the nuptial quarters, or the *numphon*, is mirrored in our present-day custom of carrying the bride over the threshold. The idea was that such an entry was a definite demarcation, a starting place. Indeed, for the young groom and bride who might not have seen each other for a year's time—who perhaps had never met at all—the entry into this little mansion was surely a genesis-site of their lives. It was a place where their union would be created.

There, for the first time, the groom would remove his bride's veil and see her and speak to her with no barriers. There, too, their marriage would be consummated. While we might be abashed and reticent about even discussing this event, the Jews were not. The fact of this accomplished event was publicly acknowledged in two ways.

First of all, a garment or sheet from the bridal bed was carefully preserved. This special sheet is the one that had on it the spot of blood that demonstrated that the bride's hymen had

been broken and that she was thus a virgin up to that point (see
Deuteronomy 22:13–19).

Secondly, the entire wedding party waited in an outer room
for news that the marriage had been consummated. Here is where
the friend of the bridegroom, his trusted companion, played a
very important role. While the other guests were further away,
the friend of the bridegroom would listen carefully for the
groom's confirming voice.

We need not suppose that this was done in a whisper, but
rather a shout of triumph, of approval of her beauty and worth.
The friend of the bridegroom would recognize that he had indeed
carried out his task of assuring the safe delivery of a chaste bride
to her husband.

"The friend of the bridegroom," John the Baptist said,
"who stands and hears him, rejoices greatly because of the bridegroom's voice" (John 3:29). Thus satisfied, the friend of the
bridegroom would announce the marriage to the waiting guests,
and the rejoicing would begin.

### Meanwhile, Outside. . . .

The bridegroom would then serve the bride a special "marriage
supper" (not to be confused with the later marriage feast) there in
his little mansion from among the provisions he had stored there.
In this, his "banquet hall," his love would surround and drape
over her like a banner (Song of Solomon 2:4). The promises he
would make to her concerning their future life together would be
ratified by a pinch of salt, referred to as "the covenant of salt,"
which would be witnessed by the presence of a few selected
friends.

The bride and groom would stay in their little mansion for
most of the marriage celebration. But meanwhile, outside, the
bridegroom's shout was the signal for festivities that would go on
for as long as a week. Of course, most of the guests would have to
attend to daily duties, but especially in the cool of the evening the
guests would return and celebrate. For this reason, the late fall
was a favorite time for weddings because the clement weather and
diminished agricultural tasks made for more time for jubilation.

According to Vine, the special group of men known as "the friends of the bridegroom" (Matthew 9:15, Mark 2:19; Luke 5:34) had charge of providing for what was necessary for the nuptials. Someone was assigned the position of "master of the banquet," and he, as we see in John 2 at the wedding at Cana, was in charge of making sure that the wine was plentiful.

Servants would make sure that each guest was properly greeted by having their feet washed with water from the great stone water jars holding twenty to thirty gallons of water (John 2:6). Those who were strict in observing the rabbinical law would in addition wash their hands repeatedly from this water. There were embraces and kisses (in this culture, a sign of reconciliation and restoration) in profusion. In a time when such celebrations and religious holidays were perhaps the only relief from a life of hard work, these people took their entertainment very seriously. Men and women were separated, but that hardly hindered the festive spirit.

What we would call the bride and groom's honeymoon was more like a week-long open house where friends and relatives stayed at the groom's father's home. The bride and groom would occasionally emerge from their private chamber to greet guests and participate in the activities. During this time they were literally treated as a king and queen, addressed as such, and even sat on thrones especially brought to the house for that purpose.

There were musicians who played favorite songs (Genesis 31:27), and singing was an important element of the celebration. Many Biblical authorities believe that the Song of Solomon was a collection of "mini-songs" that were chosen from when singing at a bridal celebration, but those under the age of thirty were forbidden to listen to or read the lyrics. Nonetheless, even the shiest maiden had a song to sing (Psalm 78:63). Dancing, too, played a part (Song of Solomon 6:13b, Judges 21:21).

From the record of the wedding of Samson in Judges 14 we can see other activities that were present. Host and guests alike would propose riddles, play games, and take part in competitions of skill. Prizes were often promised, and this atmosphere of friendly contention, along with the free-flowing wine, made for high spirits and joviality.

I attended a modern-day counterpart of such a wedding in
Nagpur, India a few years ago. It was like a combination of a wedding and a great family reunion and homecoming. Everything was
decorated with banners and festoons; and games, riddles, and
singing abounded. Though the celebration had an announced beginning, it was only ended when the provisions and money of the
host ran out.

## The Wedding Feast

The Jewish host, though, tried to keep his guests happy and full
for the whole week they were there. We can understand how
serious a thing it was to run out of wine as we read John's account
of the wedding at Cana, and marvel at how richly Jesus solved a
social problem that would have been a humiliation to the bride
and groom.

At the close of the week, however, the father of the bridegroom pulled out all the stops in providing a rich feast for all his
guests. A wealthy host, such as a king, would even provide special
"feast robes" for attendees (Matthew 22). A proctor would be
positioned at the door to hand out these robes and to guarantee
that no one who was unsuitably dressed could enter.

Again, the men and women would be separated, and as in
all Jewish dining functions, seating arrangements were crucial.
Jesus' teaching about not taking the best seat at a banquet (lest
a more honored guest than you arrive and be given your place)
had as its setting a wedding feast (Luke 14:8). Undoubtedly there
was a great deal of jockeying for the best position, and conse-
quential conclusions were drawn from the results.

All fasting and other signs of sorrow were to be put away at
the appearance of the bride and bridegroom. They emerged a
final time from their chamber to greet their guests and to partake
with them from the most sumptuous meal the father could
provide. This meal marked the beginning of a life of rejoicing
together as husband and wife, part of the community.

## The Marriage of the Lamb

You will remember that the bride's companions would sit in the
quiet evenings before the bridegroom came, singing to each

other and encouraging one another with the assurance that he would, indeed, come. It is no coincidence that the passage in 1 Thessalonians 4 which tells us the details of the Lord's return ends with the admonition, "Therefore, encourage each other with these words."

Christ's return, that passage also tells us, will be as unmistakable and joyous as the wedding procession. It will serve as a delineator of the prepared and the unprepared, but all will witness it.

There, under the *huppah* of the eternal skies, the entire world will witness Jesus' presence with His bride, the church. She will be rejoicing at this glad reunion.

But not everyone will react with this same joy. "Look, he is coming with the clouds," we read in the Revelation, "and every eye will see him, even those who pierced him; and all the peoples of the earth will mourn because of him" (1:7).

There will indeed be a consummation of the bride's marriage to the Lord. What form this will take, we do not know. But in a private place, His bride will be unveiled, and He will see her in all her beauty. Paul, and John the Baptist, and indeed all the prophets of God who predicted that moment, will be filled with joy when they realize that their labor was not in vain and that the bride will have been safely delivered to her Husband.

There the firelike eyes of the Bridegroom will burn away all the wood-hay-and-stubble imperfections we would so desperately want gone.

He will provide a wedding supper, Revelation 19:9 tells us. There the bride will feast on all the love He has stored up for us for all eternity as He prepared that bridal mansion for us. We'll have our time, alone, with Him.

And then the Father will provide the final celebration—the great feast spoken of in Matthew 22. Many will be called, but few will be chosen. Though He will actively seek our fellowship it will just be a continuation of the seeking process He has been engaged in for thousands of years (John 3:23). There will be those who will think to come into the rejoicing without preparation, without the garment He provides, but they shall be cast out into outer darkness, to a condemnation that will, by its justice, leave even the harshest critic speechless.

We want to assure ourselves that we will not be garmentless. We want to guarantee that we will be there at that feast, as bride and honored guest. Surely that will be, we tell ourselves.

But a nagging thought at the back of our minds will not be stilled. What if the bride is not found to be a virgin? Then there will be no Bridegroom's shout of triumph and approval, no feasting, no celebration. We apprehend with a crash the thought that we are the bride, and we know us, and we are not pure.

What will happen when He takes us to Himself and unveils us and knows that we have not been completely faithful to Him as we waited?

"Christ loved the church," Ephesians 5 tells us, "and gave Himself up for her, to make her holy, cleansing her by the washing of water through the word, and to present her to Himself as a radiant church, without stain or wrinkle or any other blemish, but holy and blameless."

Holy. Blameless.

How can this be, when we know we gave ourselves to the world long before we knew Him? What, we urgently ask, of the garments and bedclothes that will not be stained?

Oh, they'll be stained—not with the blood of the bride, but with the blood of the chivalrous Groom. His blood will cover for eternity this and every other infidelity we have ever committed.

# Chapter 10

## *Awaiting the Shout*

This is a love story, pure and simple.

It is the story of two lovers: Christ and His bride. We as the church see ourselves as that bride. But alongside that imagery in the New Testament is what seems to be a contradiction—for we know that we are not only His spouse, but we are also His body.

Is there a confusion of images?

Not at all. In this marriage, as in all others, the great wonder is that of how two can become one flesh. There is no confusion, only the great mystery of union.

Jews call a wedding "a building of joy," and the imagery fits our marriage with Christ, too. We can almost hear it—the hammering's slowing rhythm that tells our hearts that the Bridegroom's return is near.

Just before He left, Jesus assured His disciples that not only was He going to provide a mansion for them, but that they knew the way (John 14:4). Just by knowing the Bridegroom, we have all we need for this life and for godliness (2 Peter 1:3). We haven't been left here to muddle our own way home.

Modern-day Jews tell of a delightful tradition with the belief that when a couple marries, all their previous sins are forgiven. Thus they start their life together with "a clean slate." For us, each day brings that joy of a new beginning, for the blood of our Bridegroom cleanses us after each and every sin.

As each spiritual "Wednesday" comes and goes in our lives, we find our focus turning inward, to ourselves, and the agony we feel as we await His coming. But we are quickly humbled by the memory of Jesus, praying in the garden, with sweat drops like blood, and we know that His agony was over a bride who by her very nature could not be completely faithful to Him.

He even asked to have the cup of the marriage covenant taken away. But He didn't want an escape valve, a way out. He wanted the bride. He was willing to trust His Father to work out the details, to keep her pure.

The betrothal would be a trying time. He knew there would be paramours competing for her attention—false teachers who would flirt with her and try to take her eyes off Him. All around her would be the temptations of the immediate, ranging from annoying distractions to alluring mirages of happiness.

He knew that she would face discouragement and ridicule, because others would not understand her devotion to Him—like the daughters of Jerusalem in Song of Solomon 5:9 who just would not love Him like the bride would.

And He knew the bride would have "internal" problems, too. She would have body parts that would misbehave, always at the wrong time, and illnesses caused by dysfunctions of other parts. But as 1 Corinthians 12 tells us, each part is necessary and important. A bride awaiting her Beloved doesn't cut off an infected finger, or gouge out an afflicted eye. She nurses each back to health so that she can be complete for her Husband.

He has left us a love letter, His Word. The bride who loves Him will hang on every tender phrase and hide it in her heart. Our opportunities for intimate moments with Him are rare—but how we must treasure those times when we taste His flesh and blood, or listen attentively to His messages in our hearts.

Our wedding to Him will be a festival like never seen before. And like the bridegrooms of the Old Testament, He will devote Himself to us. We will be His full-time agenda, for eternity, a never-ending honeymoon of delight.

For us, the church, the honored Bride of Christ, the waiting is hard. Like Paul, we face the daily desire to depart and be with Him, right now. But we know we have responsibilities here that we must attend to during our lifetime of betrothal.

But it's all or nothing, this coming wedding day.

Either He will shout His approval of us, or He will remain eternally a bachelor, for we are His only love.

# Bibliography

Andrews, Samuel J., *The Life of our Lord upon the Earth*. Grand Rapids: Zondervan Publishing House, 1954.

Bailey, Albert E., *Daily Life in Bible Times*. New York: Charles Scribner's Sons, 1943.

Barclay, William, *The Daily Study Bible Series*. Philadelphia: Westminister Press, 1975.

Bouquet, Alan C., *Everyday Life in New Testament Times*. New York: Charles Scribner's Sons, 1954.

Bowen, Barbara M., *Strange Scriptures that Perplex the Western Mind*. Grand Rapids: Wm. B. Eerdmans Publishing Co., 1940.

Brav, Standley Rosebaum, *Marriage and Jewish Tradition*. New York: Philosophical Library, 1951.

Burder, Samuel, *Oriental Customs*. Philadelphia: William Woodward Publisher, 1807.

Burrows, E. P., *Sacred Geography and Antiquities*. New York: American Tract Society, 1954.

Carcopino, Jerome, *Daily Life in Ancient Rome*. New Haven: Yale University Press, 1940.

Cornell, Carl Heinrich, *Culture of Ancient Israel*. New York: 1914.

Deen, Edith, *Family Living in the Bible*. New York: Harper and Row, 1963.

*Dictionary of Christ and the Gospels*, Vol. II. James Hastings, John Selbie, John C. Lambert, editors. Edinburgh: Charles Scribner's Sons, 1921.

Edersheim, Albert, *The Life and Times of Jesus the Messiah*, Two Volumes. New York: Longmans, Green, and Co., 1905.

Eichler, Lillian, *The Customs of Mankind*. New York: Nelson Doubleday Inc., 1924.

*Encyclopedia Judaica*, Volumes 4, 6, 11. Jerusalem: Keter House Ltd./ Macmillan Co., 1971.

Epstein, Louis M., *Marriage Laws in the Bible and the Talmud*. Cambridge: Harvard University Press, 1942.

Fish, Henry, *Bible Lands Illustrated*. Hartford: American Publishing Co., 1876.

Freeman, James, *Manners and Customs of the Bible*. Plainfield, N.J.: Logos International, 1972 (reprint).

Gaster, Theodor H., *Customs and Folkways of Jewish Life*. New York: W. Sloane Associates, 1955.

Gilbertson, Merrill T., *The Way It Was in Bible Times*. Minneapolis: Augsburg Publishing House, 1959.

Goldstein, Sidney Emmanuel, *The Meaning of Marriage and Foundations of the Family*. New York: Bloch Publishing Co., 1942.

Gower, Ralph, *The New Manners and Customs of Bible Times*. Chicago: Moody Press, 1987.

Grelot, Pierre, *Man and Wife in Scripture*. New York: Herder and Herder, 1964.

Heaton, E. W., *Everyday Life in Old Testament Times*. New York: Charles Scribner's Sons, 1956.

*International Bible Dictionary*. Plainfield, N.J.: Logos International, 1977 (reprint).

*Israel in Pictures*. Visual Geography Series. New York: Sterling Publishing Co., 1962.

Jeremias, Joachim, *Jerusalem in the Times of Jesus*. Philadelphia: Fortress Press, 1989.

The Jewish Catalogue. Richard Siegel, Michael and Sharon Strassfeld, editors. Philadelphia: The Jewish Pub. Society of America, 1973.

Kennett, R. H. *Ancient Hebrew Social Life and Custom as Indicated in Law, Narrative, and Metaphor*. London Publishing for the British Academy by H. Milford, Oxford University Press, 1933.

Klinch, Arthur W. *Home Life in Bible Times*. St. Louis: Concordia Publishing House, 1947.

Latner, Helen, *Your Jewish Wedding*. Garden City: Doubleday and Co., Inc., 1985.

Leenhardt, M., *Dowry Systems among Primitive People*. Int. R. Mission, Ap. 30, Vol. 19.

Levitt, Zola, *A Christian Love Story*. Dallas: Zola Levitt, 1978.

Lamsa, George M., *Idioms in the Bible Explained and A Key to the Original Gospel*. San Francisco: Harper and Row Publishers, 1985.

Mace, David Robert, *Hebrew Marriage*. New York: Philadelphia Library, 1953.

*National Geographic*. "In the Birthplace of Christianity," "Among the Shepherds of Bethlehem." Volume 50, December 1926.

*National Geographic*. "Where Jesus Walked" by Howard LaFay. Volume 132, December 1967.

Parrot, Andrea, *Land of Christ.* Philadelphia: Fortress Press, 1968.

Patterson, Harriet Louise, *Come with Me to the Holy Land.* Valley Forge, Pa.: Judson Press/Valley Forge Press, 1963.

Pierce, Joe E. *Understanding the Middle East.* Rutland, Vt.: Charles E. Tuttle Co., 1971.

Pillai, K. C. *Light through an Eastern Window.* New York: Speller and Sons, 1963.

———. *The Orientalisms of the Bible.* Fairborn, Ohio: Munkus Publishing Co., 1969.

Reimer, Jack (editor), *Jewish Reflections on Death.* New York: Schocken Books, 1974.

Rihbany, Abraham Mitrie, *The Syrian Christ.* New York: Houghton Mifflin, 1910.

Schauss, Hayyim, *The Lifetime of a Jew Throughout the Ages of American Jewish History.* New York: Cincinnati, Union of Hebrew Congregation, 1950.

Scherer, George H., *The Eastern Colour of the Bible.* London: The National S. S. Union, 1932.

Siegel, Strossfeld, *The Jewish Christology.* Philadelphia: Jewish Publishing House.

Thompson, J. A., *Handbook of Life in Bible Times.* Madison, Wisconsin: Intervarsity, 1986.

Thomson, William M., *The Land and the Book.* Three Volumes. New York: Harper and Brothers, 1880.

Trever, John C., *Cradle of Our Faith: The Holy Land.* U.S. Junior Chamber of Commerce, 1954.

Troke, James Allen, *What a Sunday School Teacher Should Know about Palestine.* Butler, In.: Higley Press, 1942.

Wells, James, *Travel Pictures from Palestine.* New York: Dodd Mead Co., 1896.

Wilmeth, P. D. *The Christian Home.* Nashville: 20th Century Christian, 1955.

Wight, Fred H. *Manners and Customs of Bible Lands.* Chicago: Moody Press, 1953.

Wright, G. Ernest et. al, editors, *Great People of the Bible and How They Lived.* Pleasantville, N.Y.: Reader's Digest Association, 1974.

# Notes

# Notes

# Notes

# Notes

# Notes

# Notes